When Arthur Met Maggie

for Amelia Carys

Patrick Hannan
When Arthur Met Maggie

seren

Seren is the book imprint of
Poetry Wales Press Ltd
57 Nolton Street, Bridgend, Wales CF31 3AE,
www.seren-books.com

ISBN 1-85411-422-0

A CIP record for this title is available from
the British Library.

The publisher works with the financial assistance of the
Welsh Books Council.

Printed in Plantin by Cromwell Press, Trowbridge

CONTENTS

ACKNOWLEDGEMENTS

Many people helped me with this book but I'm particularly grateful to Branwen Weekes for her permission to quote extensively from the diary kept by her late husband, Philip. It is passionate, partisan, revealing, shrewd and, frequently, extremely funny; everything a diary ought to be. It contains the reflections of someone who was often at the heart of events during the miners' strike of 1984-85 and so contributes hugely to our understanding of those tumultuous days. As I read I could hear Philip speaking, and recalled the decades of friendship I had been lucky enough to enjoy with him and Branwen. Philip had no more loyal colleague and friend than Mike Meredith who, as the man in charge of public relations in the South Wales coalfield, somehow managed for decades to combine both the interests of the National Coal Board and those of the journalists who reported its affairs. He too has given me matchless assistance. I have taken some material from the series, *The Clash*, that I made for Radio Wales in 2004. I'm very grateful to BBC Wales for permission to quote freely from it. *The Clash* was a team effort and, as I have in many other projects, I relied very much on the editorial and technical expertise of the producer, Mark Palmer, and later on that of another producer, Aled Rowlands, who's also been an invaluable collaborator. Many of those whose words I use are acknowledged in the text, but I must offer particular thanks to a group of people I consulted more than once: Professor Deirdre Beddoe, Hywel Francis MP, Kim Howells MP and Siân James MP. Ursula Masson was kind enough to let me see her work on the life of Mrs Rose Davies, which I found very helpful. I've also spent a lot of time in conversation with people who have generously shared their knowledge and opinions of the matters dealt with here but who will be better served by my maintaining their anonymity. Nevertheless their contribution has been vital. Once again Penny Fishlock has saved me from the consequences of the many mistakes, repetitions and idiocies that were contained in my original manuscript. Her skills as a copy editor and the authority of her green biro are justly admired. For example, when I described Jesse James as having been shot in the back while hanging a picture, who else would have tactfully pointed out that the outlaw was actually *straightening* the picture when the fatal bullet struck? All errors that remain are entirely my responsibility. This book and much of its subject matter have taken up a substantial part of my time over a period of something like two years. It's a process that has inevitably involved moods of preoccupation and distraction of which the chief interpreter has inevitably been my wife, Menna. Her encouragement and the wide knowledge she has brought to an analysis of what I have written have been, as always, an irreplaceable component of the whole enterprise. Her contribution to the book and everything that surrounds it cannot be overstated.

INTRODUCTION

ALL GOVERNMENTS NEED ENEMIES. If there are not enough to go round they have to invent them, or at least select adequate-sounding substitutes. It is why they talk constantly of war: the war on drugs, the war on crime, the war on poverty and so on. It is the language of leadership, resolution and moral authority in which politicians like to cloak themselves. In this regard real wars can turn out to be a considerable problem, as George Bush and Tony Blair discovered soon enough in Iraq. Keep your wars metaphorical might have been the lesson they learnt the hard way from that adventure.

Margaret Thatcher was rather more fortunate in both the real and virtual aspects of warfare. Her decision in 1982 to confront Argentina over its invasion of the Falkland Islands was a risky business. It might have had disastrous consequences, not least because the vast majority of the British public were either ignorant of, or indifferent to, the question of who should exercise sovereignty over a territory containing a small number of people and a large number of sheep thousands of miles away in the South Atlantic. The evidence is, indeed, that Mrs Thatcher herself, although fired up by the sheer affront of the Argentinian seizure, was by no means as gung ho at that time as her reputation now implies. As it turned out, though, the Falklands campaign was the single most important event in the creation of her legend and her international reputation as the Iron Lady.

The electoral dividend of that conflict was paid out the following year in the form of a Conservative majority of 144. Another year after that and she was ready to fight another war, although that's not what it was called at the time. It was much more central to the future of the United Kingdom than the argument about whose flag should fly over the government buildings in Port Stanley. The Argentinians, she explained, had been the enemy without; now she was turning her fire on the people she described as the enemy within: the National Union of Mineworkers. Arresting though that statement was, something even more telling lay behind it. Although it wasn't presented in such vivid terms at the time, what she was also fighting was the class war and what we can now see was its last battle on British soil.

That battle was the long and fierce miners' strike that lasted almost exactly a year from the day it began in March 1984. Only much later was it possible to grasp the huge significance of the bitterly fought dispute, but I think the opposing leaders, Margaret Thatcher and Arthur Scargill, always understood that what was at stake was the political future of the United Kingdom. And it's clear the reason it took the course it did was due almost entirely to the implacable natures of those two people.

Arthur Scargill had also enjoyed what you might call his Falklands moment when, in 1972, he led the pickets at the West Midlands Gas Board's coke works at Saltley in Birmingham. That incident entered industrial folklore and formed an essential element in the creation of the mythology of Arthur Scargill. He didn't talk of war, of course, but the vocabulary of the left has its equivalent. Their word is struggle, with all its implications of oppressed people fighting for freedom as best they can. In such ways there was a lot in common between the chief characters in this drama: in particular that they were both dismissive of the established conventions of relationships between governments and the trade unions. Each in their own way represented a break with the past and the traditions they had sprung from. Mrs Thatcher was the radical, Arthur Scargill the conservative, even if he was a revolutionary conservative.

I think we can be pretty sure, if not absolutely certain, that they never met physically, that they were never in the same room, probably never even saw each other, except as pictures on the television screen. Sir Bernard Ingham, Mrs Thatcher's chief press secretary during her entire period as Prime Minister, generously took the time to look into the matter. Neither he nor Lady Thatcher believes that such an encounter, however brief, had ever taken place. I tried to put the same question to Arthur Scargill. An official of the Socialist Labour Party, of which Scargill is General Secretary, told me he'd passed on my e-mail, but only silence ensued.

But then, of course, Mrs Thatcher never *met* General Leopoldo Galtieri, the President of Argentina during the Falklands

War, but, as with Scargill, their confrontation took on another meaning of the word – the sense in which you might say that Wellington met Napoleon at Waterloo. Arthur's political philosophy met Maggie's in a thunderous clash that resolved many of the outstanding questions about the relationships between governments and the unions that had been at the heart of domestic political conflict in Britain throughout the twentieth century.

More than that, the two main actors not meeting is illuminating in itself. They were both contemptuous of the chats and winks and nods and deals and fixes, the industrial diplomacy that had kept the show more or less on the road for generations. Not much more than a decade previously, in the summer of 1973, Scargill's predecessor, Joe Gormley, sat in the garden of No.10 Downing Street with the then Prime Minister, Edward Heath, and the Cabinet Secretary, Sir William Armstrong.

Gormley wrote in his autobiography: "My executive didn't know about it; the Cabinet didn't know about it." The Prime Minister was thinking about his pay policy, Gormley was thinking about another big pay rise, 35 per cent in fact, for the miners.

"Well, Joe," said the Prime Minister. "What are the chances this year?"

What could be more cosy? But Margaret Thatcher would have regarded such a discussion, such a relationship, as an abdication of authority. Arthur Scargill would have looked on it as a betrayal. Each separately tore up the maps that had for so long guided official antagonists in search of a deal. From time to time some of those previously involved might have got lost, as Heath was to do a matter of months after that Downing Street conversation, but nevertheless there were plenty of well-known routes to safety. The interesting thing is that, after 1985, no one from any party tried to re-establish such a system.

In such ways the long miners' strike altered the nature of the political debate in Britain and at the same time underlined how radically the terms of that debate had been rewritten. Within months of it ending it was possible to see its impact in a new Labour attitude to the unions. In its turn that was eventually to transform the party organisation from dereliction on the skid row of politics into a sleek, election-winning machine. Mrs Thatcher probably saved Labour by striking the blow it couldn't strike itself. Nor was it the first or last time that she did such a thing. And when we consider that, we can also see how, in the process, what looked like the ultimate triumph of militant Conservatism in 1985 actually contained the seeds of that party's subsequent decline.

That was because it forced Labour to reinvent itself and to settle, for a period at least, the kind of philosophical arguments that had divided the party for almost the entire post-War period. Those arguments can be seen in the careers of two contrasting people, Aneurin Bevan and Roy Jenkins, whose contributions to British political history were perhaps not precisely what people have persistently asserted them to be. In some ways that have gone largely unnoticed, the two men were remarkably similar; for that reason they represent the persistent tensions between Left and Right at least as vividly as did the contrast between Arthur Scargill and Margaret Thatcher.

Even now, getting on for half a century after his death, plenty of people in the Labour Party still look to Aneurin Bevan as an inspiration. For them Bevan's example defines much of what is virtuous about socialism. But at the very end of his life even the factionalist Bevan had to seek unity within the party, making peace with Hugh Gaitskell in an effort to change the relentless arithmetic of the ballot box. He remains a popular figure whose words are still quoted, even by rock bands. In contrast, another miner's son from the Monmouthshire valleys, one of Gaitskell's greatest admirers and perhaps as influential a politician as Bevan, is often regarded with hostility as someone who in any number of ways betrayed his political and social origins. Yet it's Roy Jenkins's influence that can be seen in the shape of modern Labour far more than that of the magnetic Bevan.

The lives of these two quite remarkable men also raise tantalising questions about the inevitability of political and social evolution and, in particular, how much individuals matter in that process. Bevan was only 62 when he died. If he had lived, it's at least possible that he would have led his party. Even if he had not, you're bound to conclude that, with his presence, the nature of the Labour governments of the sixties would have been different. In the same way, too, there were times when Jenkins might have become Prime Minister. As he himself reflected, it could have been a flaw in his character, a lack of steel, as much as the circumstances of the time that prevented him doing so. What, you can't help wondering, would have become of Labour then? As it turned out

Jenkins was one of the founders of the Social Democratic Party, the very existence of which had, with the miners' strike, an incalculably large influence on the creation of New Labour.

The stories of Jenkins and Bevan, their origins separated by a few miles and a quarter of a century, and the philosophical divisions between them, throw light on today's Labour Party. In particular they tell us a great deal about the course of one aspect of modern British history. By slightly different routes they emerged from the kind of place and the kind of industrial background that helped define the boundaries of political debate. In the public imagination the miners, perhaps more than any other single group of people, represented one side of the economic and social divide across which workers and owners had contemplated each other.

By 1985 the reality was that the kind of social organisation represented by the mass employment of the great industries had already been dismantled. There might still have been 175,000 people employed in coal mining in the UK, but since the fifties, when the figure was 700,000, the story was one of decline. Other big nationalised employers, like steel, had lost tens of thousands of jobs in the previous few years. That last strike did two central things: it demonstrated, in the most theatrical possible way, how much a world had already been rearranged; and it revealed with brutal clarity that the changes would not cease.

The consequence of that seems to have been to push us off into some kind of post-political world in which people have been entirely unable to replace the dynamic created by the familiar relationships between governments and the governed, employers and employees. In different ways its impact can be seen everywhere, most notably among workers and their unions but also, as the nature of work has changed, in the altered role of women, for example. Most of all, though, it has emerged through the influence it has had, directly or indirectly, on the political parties as they have abandoned the traditional certainties that gave them their momentum. Now they seek to tease out ideas of a less absolute nature. They seek new places to do it, too, as the redrawing of the constitutional map of the United Kingdom makes power apparently more accessible, but perhaps more elusive than ever.

These are matters that I explore in this book, particularly in the light of the consequences of the historic year of confrontation between Arthur and Maggie, as one struggled to insist on the authority of the past and the other to deny it. The result is that political ideology as we understood it for so long has joined religious belief as the quaint preoccupation of a forgotten era. Now it is preached passionately only by a minority of strident evangelicals. This is disturbingly reflected in the growing lack of public interest in the system by which we are governed and, perhaps, in who is actually doing the governing. There is an ominous gap in the connection people make between the ballot box and what their lives are like. The class war is over and politicians and those who elect them are bereft of something to put in its place.

FRATERNALLY YOURS

WELL, YOU COULD HAVE knocked me down with one of Tony Benn's tea bags. To suggest I was startled would have been like saying that the outlaw Jesse James got a bit of a surprise when he was shot in the back while straightening a picture. Life had been reorganised even more than I had believed.

The occasion for this reflection was in May 2005 when large numbers of BBC staff went on strike and took to the picket lines as a protest against proposed job cuts. I was taken aside by a colleague, a mature man with a haunted expression.

"Do you know," he said, "that a lot of these people didn't realise that they wouldn't actually get paid for the days they're on strike? They thought... well, I don't know what they thought... but they don't seem to know what a strike *is*."

It was a bit of a facer. Here we were in a society in which the traditions of industrial dispute had long been as firmly woven into the cultural fabric of life as were rugby and male voice choirs; perhaps even more authentically than the sport and the music. Now, though, no one spoke the language any more. Who now could tell you the difference between a scab and a blackleg? Who would be able to distinguish with any confidence those gradations that took you from wildcat strike to walk-out to lock-out to working to rule to mandatory meeting to the most subtle official protest of them all, working without enthusiasm?

Indeed, so far had we come from these traditions that the trade unions themselves had started talking in Latin, often a sign of an uncertain grip on real life. They had adopted names like *Amicus* and *Unison* so that no one could be entirely sure what they did and whom they represented. The craggy acronyms of the past like NUPE and NALGO and COHSE (pronounced cosy) had been swallowed up for ever. The word worker had been almost entirely expunged from the lexicon of organised labour. Did anyone in this world any longer use the expression comrade? Did official letters still begin with the salutation "Dear Sir & Brother" and end "Yours faithfully and fraternally", as was once common practice. I saw a letter in the paper from a man called Steve Kemp. Never heard of him, I thought, but then it turned out that he was National Secretary of the National Union of Mineworkers. Not all that long ago such a person would have been recognised throughout Britain by his surname alone.

And as for those people in the BBC who didn't know what a strike was... they were employed by one of the largest and greatest journalistic organisations in the entire world. Even so, the idea had apparently passed them by that an employer might withhold your money if, instead of turning up for work, you stood outside denouncing it; not only that, but they seemed to think it was a bit unsporting, really. Odd, too, that they should have been unaware of this convention given that they were in an industry in which the technical unions, overwhelmingly so in ITV, had once possessed any amount of swagger, interpreting the texts of rule books and agreements with all the chilly and unbending expertise of a Vatican theologian.

In any case, even those not in trade unions were immersed in these specialised traditions of conflict. After all, this was what much of mainstream politics was about, in a watered-down kind of way. It was, too, indelibly part of an image of Britain in which these two sides were assumed to be conducting a largely non-violent campaign in which each tried to take advantage of the other. Workers worked as little as possible, employers squeezed them as hard as they could. It was part of the everyday currency of what we were supposed to be like.

For generations the legendary idleness and intractability of the average British worker had been familiar ingredients of film and television comedy. His (less often her) willingness to down tools at the slightest provocation, or no provocation at all, the insistent implementation of the small print of contracts and agreements, the skiving, the fiddling, the endless tea breaks, the Stalinist shop stewards, the blowing of a whistle to stop the production line, the strident call of "Everybody out", were entertainingly portrayed by people like Miriam Karlin in *The Rag Trade* on television, and by Peter Sellers in the very successful 1959 film, *I'm All Right Jack*. The jokes worked because audiences understood that they weren't some far-fetched and farcical account of factory life but, like all the best humour, got their effect from being only a slightly heightened version of what really went on.

At the same time employers were usually portrayed even less sympathetically. Heartless, greedy and often vicious (especially the young master, according to the traditions of popular fiction) or in some cases comically inept. In *I'm All Right Jack*, for example, the boss figures are mostly crooked, except for their naïve managerial fall-guy who is terminally dim. In the great Ealing comedy, *The Man in the White Suit*, still regularly broadcast on television, unions and management are equally appalled when an other-worldly scientist, played by Alec Guinness, invents a fabric that never gets dirty and never wears out. Their joint self-interest excludes any consideration of possible benefits to anyone but themselves. These satires were genially done, even if they had more than a little edge to them, but it's worth remembering that popular culture doesn't have to be accurate in every detail to give you a useful idea of social attitudes at the time they portray.

But then, suddenly, as on that day in May 2005, you realise that you might as well have been watching *Carry On Up the Khyber* for all the relevance these ideas continue to have to contemporary life. It isn't simply that things have moved on a bit. It's as if, during a brief period of inattention, someone had sneaked in and dismantled many of the structures that supported your understanding of the kind of society in which you lived. Of course this is an inevitable part of the process of getting older, but there's more to it than that.

Many of the significant changes that took place in the last two decades of the twentieth century, and spilled over into the twenty-first, have fundamentally altered our experience of the world and our understanding of our place in it. The end of the Cold War, nihilistic terrorism brought to our doorsteps, economic globalisation, a heightened sense of environmental impermanence, a revolution in communications, both in the growth of information technology and the availability of cheap travel around the world, are among the developments that have swept aside old assumptions. In that context a shift in our idiosyncratic British arrangements over work, how it shapes society and the way in which relationships are ordered within it, seems to take us pretty much into fossil-hunting country.

Except for one thing. The broad questions of industrial relations dominated domestic politics for getting on for much of the last century. That is why, after all, there was such a thing as a *Labour* Party and why for most of that period the main political arguments were essentially conducted between it and the Conservatives. Or that was the theory, but we came to see eventually that the conflict was actually between organised labour and *any* government. Ted Heath put it most starkly in 1974 when he called a general election to ask specifically who ruled Britain: was it the government or the National Union of Mineworkers. The voters gave him a tentative but nevertheless fatal answer. And, although it was wrapped up in many other matters, it was essentially the same question that was put in 1979. This time there was no ambiguity about the response of the voters, made angry and disgusted by what they saw as the sheer indifference of the public sector unions to any interests but their own. During what came to be called the winter of discontent hospitals were picketed and the dead remained unburied – two powerful symbols that were to haunt the Labour Party in the succeeding years.

It marked the beginning of an era in which the stately rituals and anachronistic clothes of traditional political relationships were carted off to the museum of not-so-modern life. Some of the old weapons were flourished from time to time; the evils of capitalism, the benefits of socialism and vice versa, but they were only employed in the way that members of the Sealed Knot brandish replica seventeenth-century swords at each other as they re-enact the battles of the English Civil War. No one was going to get hurt.

In 1945 a Labour government with a huge majority, led by Clement Attlee, rebuilt the industrial structure of Britain with a sweeping programme of nationalisation. In many cases, coal, say, or the railways or the gas and electricity supply, it came to look like the natural order of things. It was a public affirmation of what Labour stood for. That's why steel, for example, was in and out of public ownership from 1951 onwards, and why the Labour government of the seventies, strapped for cash and with no major-ity to speak of, spent a lot of time and effort nationalising the moribund shipbuilding industry. Twenty years after that, and fifty years after Attlee, another Labour government with a huge major-ity expressed no interest of any kind in disturbing the arrangements under which such corporations and many, many others, had been sold off to private investors.

In 1974, when Ted Heath lost his electoral gamble with the miners, the Wilson government that succeeded him couldn't wait to turn the clock back. Out went the Industrial Relations Act and the National Industrial Relations Court and in their place came new regulations which largely restored the conditions under which the unions had previously operated. Indeed, so keen on this process was Michael Foot, the new Employment Secretary, that he proposed making it a requirement for police to stop vehicles so that pickets could talk to the drivers. Twenty-two years later, a Labour government with the authority to do what it liked in this regard, simply averted its gaze. It entirely ignored demands to repeal what were commonly known to the unions as the Thatcher penal laws which were also, as it happened, much more effective than those introduced by Heath.

Those are only two examples, although important ones, of the way in which the political climate has changed entirely. There are others going in a different direction. No Conservative government is likely to find itself able to reduce in any serious way what people see as essential components of the welfare state. The health service will remain much as it is now. Comprehensive education will not be abolished. There will not be a grammar school in every town. The Conservatives will compete with Labour to send more people to prison and both parties will ensure that Britain remains top of the premiership in the European lock 'em up league. No Labour government will propose a programme of nationalisation. As far as Europe is concerned, practically everyone will say that, things being how they are, there's nothing much to discuss at this stage, really. What will purport to be a principled argument between the parties over taxation and public spending will continue to be essentially a debate about small change.

In these circumstances you wonder why MPs wring their hands in despair when at election time people decide that, on the whole, they don't think they'll bother, thank you very much. Statistics don't tell you everything but sometimes they tell you quite a lot. In the general elections held from 1945 to 1997 the average turnout in Britain was more than 76 per cent. Abruptly, in 2001, that figure fell to under 60 per cent. A freak? Hardly. In 2005 just over 61 per cent of the voters hauled themselves off to the polls. In fact this time they didn't even have to leave the house if they didn't want to, thanks to a new regime which made postal votes widely available.

Anguished politicians declared themselves baffled by this state of affairs and, being politicians, began to think of mechanical solutions rather than underlying causes. Why not let people vote online, or by text, or in a break from drinking alcopops during happy hour, or while shopping at Tesco on a Saturday morning? Then again, they thought, the media were probably to blame because of their relentlessly negative portrayal of political life. No wonder people were, in the jargon of the day, 'disengaged', they said with that sense of relief enjoyed by politicians when they've managed to find someone else on whom to pin the blame.

In discussing this problem we are constantly admonished not to say that there's really nothing to choose between the various parties. There is a difference, we're told, even if it becomes increasingly difficult to discern; but if people think otherwise then the outcome is likely to be very much the same. It's not that people don't have passionate views, on Iraq, perhaps, or global warming or animal welfare, it's just that they have no very clear idea on how they might vote in order to advance those causes, so they save their energy for the march or the demonstration. Perhaps in Britain we have reached a political equilibrium in which we might, from time to time, be offered a choice of management consultants.

How did we get here? Respectable historians and political philosophers tend to look down on the idea that in the progress of events the points can accidentally get switched at a crucial moment sending the train off to an entirely different destination from that intended. By and large, all things being equal, *mutatis mutandis* and the rest of it, what happens is what was going to happen anyway, they say, and 'what if?' is a question to be left to the parlour game of counterfactual chit-chat. Even so, the intricacies of political life are not only fascinating in themselves but also reveal the fragility of the idea that we are simply swept along on a tide of determinism regardless of the interaction of chance and personality. Perhaps looking at great events from this perspective lets us understand them better and why, at this moment, we are where we are.

Suppose, for example, that Ted Heath hadn't called that election in 1974, or that he had called it a little earlier and won, or that he had simply done a deal with the miners? In those circumstances the course of British political history would have been drastically altered. Again, what if Jim Callaghan had, as most people expected, called an election in the autumn of 1978 rather than being forced to do so in the spring of 1979? If Mrs Thatcher had been victorious, as was very likely, then that winter of discontent would have taken on a very different character. A little later, if Denis Healey rather than Michael Foot had succeeded Callaghan, might Healey have been able to avoid the worst of the infighting that split the party, most significantly the defection of senior members to launch the Social Democrats? But Foot's leadership, notably the disaster of the 1983 election, was probably an essential prelude to the determination of the new Labour leadership, under Neil Kinnock to take on the left, chiefly the Trotskyites of the Militant Tendency, but also to limit some of the more damaging activities of the unions.

Then again, if Kinnock had won the 1992 election, as he might have and, some people say, should have, a Labour government would have faced the crisis of Black Monday and Britain's departure from the Exchange Rate Mechanism. Such events would have revived Labour's notorious reputation for economic incompetence. As a result might we then have seen, in 1996 or 1997, a new Conservative government led by John Major enjoying the economic revival that followed, rather than a Labour administration under Tony Blair doing so?

If Joe Gormley had retired as President of the National Union of Mineworkers early enough for the Communist Mick McGahey rather than Arthur Scargill to win the election to succeed him, it seems probable that the miners' strike of 1984-85 would have had a very different character. There's good reason to think that it would have ended in compromise rather than in the ashes of disaster. If one of the two leading characters in that drama – either Scargill or Mrs Thatcher – had been absent, wouldn't some less catastrophic conclusion have been reached and reached sooner? And in those circumstances would the future of the whole trade union movement and the Labour Party have been different?

Many sensible people might conclude that this sort of thing is simply profitless speculation. It didn't happen and that's that. The events of the past give us some clues at least to what might happen in the future. The peculiar state of UK politics in which many of the most important arguments take place within parties rather than between them has so disrupted the traditional debate of the previous hundred years that the distinctions we once made with familiar ease – between left and right, between Labour and Conservative even – have become much more problematical. If new arguments are to replace them then they might come from unexpected shifts and initiatives that arise from some of the events of the last quarter of century. For example, you could argue that Margaret Thatcher and Arthur Scargill were separately and in combination at least partly responsible for the creation of New Labour. It was to be an organisation that wrecked the modern Conservative Party, an outcome that in the circumstances might give Lady Thatcher some sardonic pleasure. But it also came to represent practically everything Arthur Scargill hated most in political life. It's difficult to think of a stranger outcome or, perhaps, a more entertaining one. It's a powerful illustration of the law of unintended consequences. Others have already taken place and there are certainly more to come.

OUT! OUT! OUT!

EVEN TODAY, LONG AFTER she was taken from Downing Street for the last time as Prime Minister, red-eyed and shockingly diminished, it's still possible to be rocked by the sheer hatred that the name Margaret Thatcher can arouse. You can be taken aback even in South Wales where Conservative prime ministers have traditionally been reviled down the ages, where Conservatives as a class were denounced by Aneurin Bevan as "lower than vermin". This is a place in which the vigour of people's anger, the way they keep it fresh, is quite remarkable. For more than half a century miners and their families kept up a feud with Winston Churchill because he sent troops into Tonypandy in 1910. But they didn't detest Churchill then as much as they detest Thatcher to this day. It's a feeling that's been matched throughout the old industrial areas of Britain. One of the most evocative sounds of the late twentieth century was the chant echoing through so many streets: "Maggie! Maggie! Maggie! Out! Out! Out!" I can't remember anyone chanting the name of John Major in any form. "Heath out," they called in the mighty industrial convulsions of *his* era, but somehow not with the same conviction. Outside the House of Commons one afternoon in the early seventies, thousands of demonstrators from the Shotton steelworks, on Deeside, threatened with closure, took up a chorus: "Ee aye addio, Teddy is a queer". It all seemed pretty harmless fun, really, although the then political editor of the BBC went round worrying whether, if this singing were accidentally broadcast, it might be considered actionable.

With Thatcher it's different. At the beginning, I suspect, that was because she confounded expectations, especially expectations of how a woman should behave, even more so of how a mother should behave, although her interest in the details of motherhood had famously been perfunctory. But in Wales, that socially conservative heartland of Mamolatry, the policy that first brought her to public fame was considered to be almost an outrage against nature. According to the *Sun* it made her the most unpopular woman in Britain, an interesting reputation for someone then at the threshold of her cabinet career.

The row broke out over her decision to end the provision of free school milk to eight to eleven year olds which, in many circumstances, might have passed as a relatively uncontroversial measure. After all, a Labour government had stopped free milk for secondary school children and not very much had been said about it. Nevertheless she knew she was on sensitive territory. Government papers published thirty years later showed she had tried to tone down the policy by resisting a suggestion that all free school milk should be abolished. "I think the complete withdrawal of free milk for our school children," she wrote in a memorandum, "would be too drastic a step and would arouse more public antagonism than the saving justifies."

That was to be proved a shrewd, if clinical, judgement. Even the relatively modest cut she introduced proved too much for some people. In places like industrial South Wales, after all, many people weren't even a generation away from the diseases of poverty and deprivation – tuberculosis, for example – that had been such a scourge through much of the century and before. And it was improved living conditions, including better nutrition, as much as the advance of medical science and the creation of the National Health Service, that had been the route to eliminating these diseases. Now here was a Tory government remaining true to the principles of the owners down the ages and taking food from the mouths of the poor. That's how it could be presented, anyway, and since it could be, it was.

All free school milk was eventually to be abolished, but it's significant in a Welsh context that much later, when the National Assembly was established, it was restored to primary school children. It was interesting, too, that the Welsh Assembly Government set about introducing a system of free breakfasts at school. These were measures that were as much a symbolic riposte to Mrs Thatcher after an interval of something like thirty years as they were a contribution to the welfare of the young.

In Merthyr Tydfil the local council, led by the Mayor, Gerry Donovan, achieved nationwide fame through a long campaign, often ingeniously fought, to defy the Thatcher edict. She might have banned milk, they argued at one stage, but no one said anything about milk *shakes*. It was no use, of course, but in Merthyr they still insist that they coined the slogan, "Thatcher, the Milk Snatcher", a description that was to prove indelible – not least because it was so useful to the newspapers, that catchy little rhyme, as the alliteration of Welsh windbag was to be a decade or so later.

In his biography of Margaret Thatcher, Hugo Young argued that this was an absurd issue on which to enter the national demonology. But there was an element in this that was new to British politics. "Lurking somewhere in the mix, both in her projection of herself and in the bitterly derisive responses she was capable of arousing, was the fact of her gender. For a woman to have taken milk from the mouths of needy innocents was some-how astonishingly wicked. The episode was an early instance of a continuing phenomenon: the anxieties and resentments, the over-compensation and the underestimation, flowing from her sex."

This allegation of unnatural behaviour no doubt added to the pressure on Mrs Thatcher who at this stage, after all, was a novice cabinet minister. The evidence is that it didn't frighten her, although it alarmed her husband, Denis, who, Hugo Young reported, feared for her health and suggested she might even think of getting out of politics altogether. Well, we know now, if we didn't know then, that such a surrender would have been entirely unchar-acteristic. She later agreed that she was hurt by some of the things the newspapers said about her but solved that problem by not reading them. Typically, too, she doesn't seem to have any doubt that she was right in this matter. Another biographer, Patrick Cosgrave, says that she favoured the step of cutting school milk. It was by no means something forced on her and he quotes her as telling the Conservative MP, George Gardiner: "Every depart-ment had to make some cuts but I was determined that I was not going to make mine in education itself. School milk and school meals aren't education as such. I took the view that most parents are able to pay for milk for their children, and that the job of the government was to provide such things in education which they couldn't pay for, like new primary schools."

She wrote later: "When I was at Huntingdon Road Primary School my parents paid 2½d (1p) a week for my school milk and there were no complaints. By 1970 very few children were so deprived that school milk was essential for their nourishment."

Although she probably wouldn't have been aware of it, in

taking such a tone she also raised fierce traditional antagonisms. She was speaking with the authentic voice of the lower middle class, the voice of the grocer's daughter. Bourgeois tradesmen always needed paying sooner or later and, although they often shared the same streets as their customers, some of them preferred to avert their gaze from the hardship and penury that regularly overwhelmed their communities. Mrs Thatcher's view, to judge from her comments, was that the poor weren't actually as poor as they made themselves out to be. Maybe in 1970 they weren't, but they had been within living memory, and the shopkeeper, prospering and sermonising from a rung or two up the social ladder, could be a detestable figure. Long after he had gone to serve behind the celestial counter, people, entirely unprompted, told me stories about Mrs Thatcher's father, Alderman Alfred Roberts. They described in detail how, in his Grantham shop, he would surreptitiously put his thumb on the scales while weighing out portions of haslet, a meat loaf made mainly from cooked pieces of pig's offal and as such, you'll understand, scarcely a luxury item. Such things were no doubt said about every grocer in Britain, including Mr Fortnum and Mr Mason, but they illustrate the resentments that could flourish so easily, not least in areas where working people made a serious study of the works of Karl Marx and his account of the struggle between the proletariat and the bourgeoisie.

I suppose it can hardly be considered a matter of any surprise that Mrs Thatcher attracted bile from those who could, to a greater or lesser extent, legitimately consider themselves to be economic victims of her policies. What is more arresting, though, is the way in which people in more comfortable worlds came to think of themselves as belonging to some kind of intellectual underground. There was, for example, the June 20th Group, a bunch of drawing room revolutionaries brought together by the playwright Harold Pinter and his wife, Lady Antonia Fraser. They were much given to evenings of well-fed anguish as they talked the language of bills of rights and even of the formation of a modern version of that model of thirties left wing idealism, a popular front. No doubt they dreamt of thinkers and workers marching side by side behind the banner of a canapé rampant.

In his diary entry for November 22, 1990, one of the June 20th participants, Richard (later Sir Richard) Eyre, then director of the National Theatre, wrote about travelling through Paris in a taxi and hearing that Thatcher had resigned. He and his companions cheered. Arriving at the theatre he found the whole company in a state of high jubilation: "I feel a slight sense of the 'locked door syndrome'; if she went so easily why wasn't the door pushed before. She has been an autocrat, inhibited thought, crushed imagination, but haven't we been supine?"

You might be forgiven for thinking that this reflection is rather heavy with a sense of oppression when you consider it comes from a man whose job is to spend millions of pounds of public money putting on whatever plays he and his colleagues choose without any hint of disapproval from Downing Street or, to a very large extent, from any other part of the government. Or reaction of any kind, come to that. And you might think it all the more when you realise that 'the locked door syndrome' refers specifically to a conversation Eyre had in Bucharest earlier in the year, a few months after the Romanian president, Nicolae Ceausescu, had been deposed and executed. He asks: "Do they feel guilt for not having tried to push open the door and finding it wasn't locked when they did?"

Margaret Thatcher and Nicolae Ceausescu? It isn't only the theatre you wonder about when you read such comparisons. And yet... you also have to remember that the world in which we live is so inexplicable that Ceausescu had been given an honorary knighthood in 1978, on the say-so of a Labour government run by Jim Callaghan, a distinction that was revoked by Mrs Thatcher only a matter of hours before the doomed president heard the rattle of the firing squad loading their rifles.

Such fragments underline the fact that there was, almost from the very beginning, a blizzard of hostility towards Margaret Thatcher, particularly from the old industrial areas of the country, but not only there, where she seemed to represent something unfathomably alien. Even long after she withdrew from public life she was still the object of rancorous criticism. Gleeful press coverage of her son's involvement in an African coup, an escapade that might have got him sent to gaol, was as much about her as it was about him. As late as January 2005 the *Daily Mirror* published a photograph of her, elderly, frail and confused, taken the previous day. The paper put a dotted line around the picture and the caption: "Cut this out and put it on the mantelpiece. It will keep the kids away from the fire."

You wonder if she deserves the undiluted acid of condemnation poured on her down the years? Maybe not, but for those who
insist that there's nothing to mitigate her time in office (her *régime*,
as it was often called by those who felt the word had a suitably
totalitarian flavour) there are also unspoken reasons why her
opponents still invoke her name as the essence of political menace.
One is that she provides a useful place for others to hide, Labour
politicians most prominently among them. During her time in
Downing Street the lives of many people in Britain were turned
upside down. Many of the big industrial and economic questions
over which Labour governments had agonised during the seventies had the life shaken out of them. She cut a swathe through
over-manned nationalised industries, privatised more attractive
public sector enterprises, disciplined the unions, sold off council
houses and did other things her critics would not have dared to do
themselves. They did not, though, when the time came, try and
undo them. What they could say instead was that they weren't at
the scene of the terrible crime, although they had seen a blonde
woman running off.

The reason life isn't perfect today, they like to suggest, is
because Mrs Thatcher brought a ball and crane and other items of
demolition machinery into industrial Britain. Almost fifteen years
after she left office, Rhodri Morgan, marking his fifth anniversary
as Welsh First Minister, told the press: "My own personal ambition is to try to undo the damage that Margaret Thatcher did to
Wales – that's what I have a burning ambition to do." Once again
the implication is that Mrs Thatcher was a malevolent force who
swept aside the proper concerns of ordinary people. That seems to
be an extravagant point of view but there's no doubt about one
thing. Mrs Thatcher shattered the world that was so familiar to
people like Rhodri Morgan. Whether she did so on purpose is
open to question, as we'll see. But what is incontrovertible is that
she didn't do it alone.

★

As in the lives of the saints, so in the early careers of significant
politicians, apologists look for evidence that they were somehow
given special powers of insight that allowed them to read the signs
hidden from those with less highly-tuned sensitivities. So one

popular version of the Margaret Thatcher story is that she alone of
Ted Heath's cabinet stood out against the decision to call a general
election early in 1974; that she believed a more resolute prime
minister could have confronted and defeated the NUM; and that,
soon after, she began to formulate her programme of revenge
against the miners which ended in her smashing their power once
and for all in March 1985.

That there is no evidence for any of this is largely irrelevant. The
political process is no less incoherent than the rest of life and, once
the dust has settled, there's always a temptation to impose a coherent pattern on the accidents and shifts that drive a series of events
to an inevitable conclusion. At the same time, though, you might
argue that the character of the people most intimately involved in
this affair would almost inevitably take them to the same destination,
however many detours they might make on the journey.

It seems to me that the persistence of the assertion that Mrs
Thatcher specifically provoked the strike – Mrs Thatcher's guilt, if
you like – is based less on the ascertainable facts of the case and
more on a pressing psychological need among the supporters of
the theory. As with the death of Princess Diana, for example,
everyday explanations, however plausible, simply won't do. Such a
catastrophe must have suitably awesome origins. It couldn't just
have happened. A drunken chauffeur couldn't simply have made
a terrible mistake. The National Union of Mineworkers couldn't
have stumbled its way to virtual annihilation thanks to a combination of political obsession, mistaken judgement and tactical
incompetence. Dark forces must have been at work. It was a plan,
a plot, a conspiracy. And in such cases, of course, the more it's
denied the truer it must be. The less evidence you can find, the
more obvious it is that the establishment is deeply implicated since
only people at the highest levels of authority have the necessary
resources to conceal the facts so thoroughly. How do we know that
aliens have landed on earth? Because the CIA denies it.

It's impossible to prove conclusively that Mrs Thatcher didn't
come to office bent on punishing the National Union of
Mineworkers for past crimes against the Conservative Party,
culminating in the strike that effectively drove Ted Heath's government from office in 1974. Like almost everyone else, though, she
must have understood that the only person responsible for that
defeat was Heath himself. And while the story of 1974 might well

have influenced what happened in 1984, it was because Mrs
Thatcher and her colleagues learnt from it while Arthur Scargill
and the NUM entirely misinterpreted its significance.

People who were in the Heath cabinet don't simply deny that a
desire for revenge had been secretly nurtured down the years; when
you ask them the question they look baffled. Politics is a matter of
calculation; a confrontation with Arthur Scargill, easily portrayed
as a revolutionary figure who was not even supported by large
sections of his own membership, would be an obvious strategy; but
to attack miners as a class, people for whom the public had
frequently demonstrated admiration and gratitude, would have
been crazy. And whatever else they might be, we should remember
that cabinet ministers are, by and large, not mad.

Mrs Thatcher drew important lessons from the miners' strikes
of 1972 and 1974 that so damaged the Heath government. So did
lots of other people who served in that cabinet with her. So did
Arthur Scargill, or he thought he did, although he misunderstood
in a fatal way what the lessons of that period were. Worse than that,
he seems to have failed to realise that other people were capable of
analysing those events and constructing a strategy to prevent their
repetition. Indeed, it's impossible to understand the story of 1984-
85 without knowing what had happened in the same field just over
a decade previously. Beyond that you can reach back at least into
the 1920s to discover what had even then lit a long, slow fuse that
eventually fired that last great explosion.

The strike of 1974 is supposed to have fuelled Mrs Thatcher's
specific ambition to teach the miners a lesson; it might be more
accurate to say rather that it was one of the factors that made her
determined to teach her own leader a lesson. The strike was only
the last in a series of blows and misjudgements that had buffeted
a hapless government from one crisis to another. Between them
they led directly to Mrs Thatcher's decision to challenge Heath for
the party leadership in 1975. A large part of her career as Prime
Minister was ostentatiously modelled on being as unlike her predecessor as possible. That included not giving in to the miners,
although not invariably so as we shall see, but more specifically it
meant avoiding the indecision and erratic movements of policy
that made Heath vulnerable in the first place.

Heath had come to office in 1970 determined to avoid the
course taken by his Labour predecessor Harold Wilson. Not for

him the endless acrimony of a prices and incomes policy. Not for this government the futile intervention in the affairs of lame duck companies who would now have to seek their own salvation. It didn't last long, as Geoffrey Howe told me more than thirty years later. "I never thought I'd be summoned into the Cabinet on November 6, 1972, specifically to handle and enforce a prices and incomes policy. We'd done a U-turn. We were doing what we said we wouldn't do that had failed in the hands of the Labour government before us. We did it only in despair. We were trying to cope with tearaway inflation because we'd forgotten the importance of monetary policy."

As for all those lame ducks? Well, Rolls-Royce, one of the most famous names in British industrial history, had to be saved, didn't it? So too did Upper Clyde Shipbuilders where an employee work-in seized the initiative and the public imagination. In the end the government came up with the necessary cash. Such public dramas, alongside the permanent friction involved in a prices and incomes policy, showed one fatally damaging thing: this government could be pushed around.

Added to that was something Heath and his ministers couldn't even pretend they might control. On October 6 the Arab-Israeli hostilities became the Yom Kippur war. The Arab countries attacked Israel's backers in the west by cutting oil production. Then they raised the price from $3 a barrel to $5. Two months later they more than doubled it again. Not only did this throw an enormous boulder through the window of Heath's economic strategy but overnight it made the miners, suppliers of a now vital alternative source of energy, the most powerful group of workers in the country. In these circumstances they could hardly lose but, the question still arises, did they have to win in a manner that was so spectacular that it reverberated through the political world for years to come.

The answer has to be no. Opportunities taken rather than rejected, some tactics modified only slightly, advice heeded rather than ignored might have changed the entire course of British political history in the last thirty years of the twentieth century. Mrs Thatcher's name might have been little more than a footnote in books written about other people entirely. One single event, approached differently, might have been enough to undo everything that followed.

At the beginning of 1974 the argument had come down to the

question of whether there was some way of giving the miners the money they wanted without destroying the government's fragile incomes policy. On January 9, the Chancellor of the Exchequer, Anthony Barber, was chairing a meeting of the National Economic Development Committee (known as Neddy) when Sir Sidney Greene, the General Secretary of the National Union of Railwaymen, and Chairman of the TUC's economic committee, suddenly came up with a remarkable proposition. He said that if the miners were made a special case then the other unions wouldn't use it as a precedent to advance their own pay negotiations.

It was entirely against the protocols of Neddy meetings that such a proposal should be made without any prior warning. In these circumstances Barber was taken aback and very suspicious. He had unexpectedly become Chancellor after the sudden death of Iain Macleod, and was very much a second division politician, someone without much by way of strategic insight. His first thought was that the TUC couldn't deliver on any such promise and he nipped out of the meeting to phone Heath. The Prime Minister agreed with him that the offer should be turned down. Geoffrey Howe later explained that there were any number of reasons for doing so. "The timing was awful because the offer was made on January 9 and a week later the TUC endorsed it. The following day was the last day on which Ted Heath could call an election on the old register. So everything was running against us."

James Prior, who was then Leader of the House, told me later that he thought they'd been right to reject the idea of a deal with the unions. "We'd had these offers before and when they were accepted they were never honoured. Other unions were able to get through."

Now, though, it looks as though the government, already partly mesmerised by the idea of holding a general election, and clinging on to the wreckage of most of its policies, missed an opportunity to turn the tables on the unions, including the miners. Derek Ezra, then Chairman of the National Coal Board, thought that to some extent the government had every reason to accept. "Mr Heath would have been in a very strong position. He could have said, 'I trust you'. It either would have come off or it wouldn't have. If it didn't come off then he could blame the TUC and the CBI, but my belief is it would have come off and it would have solved the problem. I think there was a general feeling then that the miners were a special case and should be treated that way."

Later, in her autobiography, Mrs Thatcher was to agree that this was the course the government should have taken, although she doesn't claim to have argued it at the time. "We might have done better to accept it and put the TUC on the spot. As it was the TUC offer undoubtedly put us on the defensive."

The key point in all this is that an agreement, even an agreement that failed, would have dealt with the problem of the NUM and all the emotional baggage that went with it. If the TUC didn't deliver, and it probably wouldn't have, it could safely have been accused of bad faith while the government went round parading its appetite for conciliation. It was also the case that there was getting on for another eighteen months to go before it would have been necessary to have a general election. By then the public mood might have been very different. So by rejecting the offer Heath and his advisers missed a chance to unload some of the blame for industrial unrest and to choose a more propitious time for an election. As it was they got the other half of the equation wrong, too, by not calling the election soon enough. The new annual electoral register was now coming into force. Conventional political wisdom at that time was that the old register – and the older the better within its one year life – gave a distinct advantage to the Conservatives. Mrs Thatcher has written that she argued for an early election and Geoffrey Howe is someone who believes that it might all have been different.

"I think that had Ted Heath called the election on the issue of who rules Britain a fortnight earlier then we should almost certainly have won and history would have been different. So either way, had we accepted the TUC offer history might have been different. If he'd called the election a fortnight earlier history might have been different."

History's like that, as Lord Howe cheerfully put it thirty years later. But one thing is blindingly clear from all this. The defeat of Ted Heath was not inevitable, even though you might argue that his character, illustrated by his failure of nerve over economic policy, made an outcome of this nature more or less inevitable at some stage. But the details of this drama and its spectacular public conclusion were his undoing. Without it, it's perfectly plausible to say, he would not have been bundled out of the leadership twelve months later; or at least not bundled out by Mrs Thatcher. More than that, who's to rule out the possibility that, at another time, in

calmer circumstances, he might have won a second term as unexpectedly as he'd won his first? And without that election, the
challenge to the voters to decide who ruled Britain, Arthur Scargill
might never have come to believe that the National Union of
Mineworkers was so powerful that governments stood or fell at its
pleasure. The miners didn't defeat Ted Heath, but the belief that
they did was for them the most damaging consequence of all the
turmoil of that grim winter. It looked like a triumph but in the long
run it turned out to be a disaster.

★

In psychiatry there is a condition described as *folie à deux* in which
two people who, left to their own devices, would be more or less
harmless, can in combination become subject to shared delusions
and bizarre and dangerous behaviour. Is this the syndrome, you
wonder, that afflicted Arthur Scargill and Margaret Thatcher so
that, after a year of bitter and violent confrontation, they were left
standing amid the wreckage of a once great industry? Have there
ever been two more intransigent opponents confronting each
other across a British domestic battlefield, each convinced of the
other's homicidal intent?

One characteristic they certainly shared: they were not like
their predecessors. More than that, they were both determined to
be as unlike their predecessors as possible. Serving in Edward
Heath's cabinet, Mrs Thatcher had seen the consequences of a
failure of resolution, especially in economic policy. When she
made her famous statement: "You turn if you want to, the lady's
not for turning", everyone understood the barbed reference to
those acrobatic reversals performed by the Heath government over
pay policy and industrial intervention.

In a similar way Arthur Scargill broke with the traditions not
only of his industry but of the entire trade union movement. All
trade union leaders had always known, even the great Communist
general secretaries of the NUM like Arthur Horner and Will
Paynter, that every dispute would eventually end in compromise.
That was how the system worked. Scargill didn't believe in that and
he had no time for the courtship rituals that attended the processes
of industrial negotiation. Kim Howells was the South Wales miners'
research officer and front man during the 1984-85 strike. He

explained how remarkable he found the Scargill approach. "Arthur was absolutely useless at negotiating. In fact I remember he used to boast that he would never go to negotiations about issues like absenteeism because he would never be seen on the side of anyone who was disciplining one of his members. That is not what trade unionism is about. It's an iconoclastic approach which, multiplied, resulted in disaster for the NUM."

An article about Scargill, written for the *Sunday Times* in 1982 by the lawyer-playwright John Mortimer, reveals how flamboyantly unpredictable his political philosophy could turn out to be. Mortimer asked him, for example, if he had left the Communist Party because of the Soviet invasion of Hungary. "Oh, no," Scargill told him. "I supported the Soviet Union over Hungary. The Hungarian revolution was joined by known fascists. No, I disagreed with the Russians not allowing dissidents to leave the country. I'd give all the dissidents free passes to get out as quickly as they could."

And there was another reason. "I also objected to the moving of Stalin's body outside the mausoleum and changing the name of Stalingrad. It would be like trying to pretend Churchill never existed. It was distorting history. And I didn't like the personal discipline of the party. They wanted me to sell the *Daily Worker* on Fridays, but I had union business to look after on a Friday so I joined the *Co-operative Party*."

At this time too, as others reported, he was always ready to give his own legend a quick polish. Mortimer wrote: "As I left he showed me the photograph of one of his most notable battles – when he joined the flying pickets outside the Saltley coke depot at the time of the great struggle against the Heath government. In the general melée he had fallen to the pavement. 'That's the only time,' he said, 'when you'll see Arthur Scargill on his knees'."

It was at the Saltley depot in Birmingham that the legend of Arthur Scargill was created. No one believed in it more fervently than he did and, perhaps, no one was more grievously misled by it than he was. It was perhaps the Agincourt of the 1972 miners' strike and, just as the longbowmen there had been the instrument of England's victory there so, in 1972, a new form of fighting man won the day for the NUM: it was then that the flying picket took his place in history.

Flying pickets were groups of men, often assembled in large

numbers, who were transported by the union to targets around the country. There were plenty of people available because there was no need to picket any collieries. A change in the industry's wages system, a move away from piecework, meant that there was now an unaccustomed unity across the British coalfields. They had not yet reached complete parity by this stage but pay rates were now close enough to mean they had a common cause – which even included Nottingham, a coalfield that had been viewed with suspicion at least since the General Strike, when it had quickly returned to work, while others stayed out for months. So no miners worked and many of them gathered at power stations, steelworks, docks, coal depots and other places where coal was being moved. It was a strategy drawn directly from the lessons of history, most powerfully from 1926. The fact that the TUC had then called the General Strike also meant that it had the power to call it off again. This time the NUM General Secretary, Lawrence Daly, had gone to the TUC general council and asked for only one specific measure of support. That its members didn't, under any circumstance, cross picket lines.

The unions co-operated with enthusiasm. The rail unions provided detailed information on coal movements so that pickets would be in the right place to challenge them. Sometimes, if pickets didn't turn up, they sent for them. Train drivers complained that at one railway bridge over the line leading to a power station at Aberthaw on the South Wales coast, they couldn't see the picket stationed there. The response was to hang a miner upside down from the bridge so that he could paint, "Stop. Miners' picket line," on its ironwork. As soon as they saw the lettering, the drivers put the brakes on.

But the most spectacular exploit of all was early in February at the Saltley coke works in Birmingham. It was important for two reasons: it made the government realise that it couldn't hope to prevail in the dispute and it made a hero of Arthur Scargill. Even before it happened Scargill seems to have had an idea that this was going to be a momentous event. Certainly that was the version told to the historian and Labour MP, Hywel Francis, by his father, Dai, the Communist General Secretary of the South Wales miners.

Arthur Scargill rang up the day before and said, "Look, Dai, we need pickets up at Saltley, in Birmingham".

Dai said: "Where's that?"

Arthur explained.

"Yes, we can organise them. When do you want them?"

"Tomorrow, Saturday."

Dai paused: "But Wales are playing Scotland at Cardiff Arms Park".

There was a silence and Scargill replied: "But Dai, the working class are playing the ruling class at Saltley".

South Wales sent pickets but they were told to buy a television *en route* to Birmingham so they wouldn't miss the game.

"My father managed to mobilise more pickets at Saltley than Arthur did," Hywel Francis said. "And they were there before his pickets. And although Arthur claimed it as a personal victory for him, it was the South Wales pickets that actually made the difference."

He paused for a moment. "At least that's what my father said."

Saltley became the focus for a mighty industrial confrontation. Other workers downed tools in their factories and joined the picket line in support of the miners. On February 10 there were 15,000 men there confronting a thousand police. It was inevitable that the police had to end the struggle and the gates to the coke works were closed. It was more than symbolic. A note containing the news was taken into a cabinet meeting. Ministers recognised that they had to look quickly for a route to a settlement. That was the day on which the Wilberforce Inquiry was established. Douglas Hurd, then Heath's private secretary, recorded in his diary: "The government is now vainly wandering over the battlefield looking for someone to surrender to, and being massacred all the time".

And, of course, one of the people at that cabinet meeting was the Education Secretary, Margaret Thatcher. She reflected later on the triumph of violence used against the state. It was, she wrote in her autobiography, "a frightening demonstration of the impotence of the police in the face of such disorder". As the gates closed at Saltley she was taking one significant lesson from these events.

At the same moment Arthur Scargill might already have been anticipating that last great confrontation that was to begin a dozen years later. He told the television cameras: "Here was living proof that the working class had only to flex its muscles and it could bring governments, employers, society to a complete standstill". And here, too, in a single sentence, was the core of Scargill's political philosophy.

This was why, twelve years later, Scargill was calling on the NUM to "tighten the knot". As the strike went on into the summer

of 1984 he claimed, entirely falsely, that coal stocks were dwin-
dling. "The quicker other industries are affected," he said, "the
quicker the government's policies will change and our people will
win the right to work." But this strategy was outdated. It was
essentially an attempt to apply the methods of 1972 and 1974 to
a world that had been radically altered.

"It was a re-run of Saltley Gate a decade before without
understanding the changed circumstances," Hywel Francis said.
"The changed circumstances were to some extent brought on by
himself in that he didn't fully understand the importance of unity
within the NUM, unity between the NUM and the wider trade
union movement and potentially a very sympathetic public. That
was all thrown to the winds and he assumed there could be a
replay of those aspects of '72 and '74 that he chose to remember,
namely the apparent effectiveness of picketing. Mass picketing in
'72 but targeted, strategic picketing in '74. But he misunderstood
that all of that was based on the very sound, solid unity of the
NUM – and that never existed in '84.

"He thought that everything could be achieved through trade
union power and the organisation of the trade union movement
without any sophistication, without any understanding that it was
a political solution at the end of the day. He thought he could bring
the government down through industrial action. He misunderstood the significance of 1974: that Mr Heath had brought himself
down by calling a general election. It wasn't the miners that
brought about the change of government, it was Heath himself
who did that."

The arrival of Scargill as president of the NUM at the end of
1981 meant an abrupt end to the inclusive culture that had characterised the relationship between management and the unions in
the industry. From now on there would be no more cosy deals like
those cooked up by his predecessor, Joe Gormley, with the coal
board Chairman, Derek Ezra, in the wood-panelled offices of
Hobart House, the NCB's Grosvenor Place headquarters. He
clearly saw his election, with more than 70 per cent of the vote, as
an opportunity not simply to advance the cause of the miners but
to strike a decisive blow in the class struggle.

Of course a lot of trade union leaders say such things, and
perhaps believe them, as they make their way up the hierarchy,
until the reality of high office reveals the limits of power and the

necessity for compromise. Joe Gormley, a skilled operator in these matters, thought very much the same sort of thing would happen to Scargill. In his autobiography he wrote: "Men tend to mellow a little when they get power. Arthur may have made a lot of promises about how he will never change his philosophies and so on and so forth, but he will find out soon enough that you can't be fighting battles all your life. There do come moments in negotiations when you have to say to yourself, 'This is all we are going to get, and there's no sense pushing for any more.' Ever since he came on the Executive Arthur was among the 'antis' who would vote against anything, but again, he will soon come to realise that if everyone votes against everything, and that happens all the time, then nothing can be achieved at all."

As a soothsayer and reader of character, we now know, Gormley was in this instance entirely wrong. Forgivably so, perhaps, because no one had ever previously seen anything like the Scargill phenomenon in the higher ranks of the trade union movement. Workplace agitators and trouble-makers, shop stewards who sometimes gained national fame for a while, behaved like this; but not presidents and general secretaries who had much wider responsibilities. If Gormley had seen it coming he might have tried to do something about it, but the reverse was true. During 1981 he told me specifically that he'd deliberately delayed his retirement so that under union rules the vice president, Mick McGahey, would be too old to stand as his successor. McGahey was an old-style Communist, but although he was one of Scargill's lieutenants during the strike, he would never have taken the NUM down the road to annihilation. That was not the Communist way, but in those days, of course, Scargill was, like Gormley, a member of the Labour Party and had to be supported in any contests with the CP.

Gormley did have some premonitions, though. Two years before he retired a meeting was held at his home to try and get agreement on someone to challenge Scargill for the presidency. The fact that the meeting had been held was leaked to the press and Gormley gave up in exasperation. "Straight away I had to tell the 'moderate' group: 'To hell with it. If we're going to be conducting this discussion in public, then I can't have anything more to do with it'."

As the time to decide the succession drew near, rank and file miners were clear enough about what should happen. "It's got to be Arthur," they would say, and then add, "but he's got to stay out of politics." At that time Kim Howells, then doing historical research, went to talk to Scargill at the Yorkshire miners' headquarters in Barnsley. Hearing his description of that encounter it's worth reflecting that at that time Kim, a member of the Communist Party, was, officially at least, to Scargill's left.

"I can remember going into his room in Barnsley – what they used to call Arthur's castle – and being really shocked. I came from a political culture which, apart from the old worship of Stalin back in the forties and fifties, had really resented the cult of the personality. I walked into Arthur's room and I saw this Mussolini desk with a great space in front of it, and behind him this huge portrait on the wall, this big painting of Arthur on the back of a lorry in this Leninist pose where apparently he was portrayed at Grunwicks* urging the working class to overthrow the oppressors.

"I thought that anyone who can put a painting like that behind his desk is nuts, and coming back down and telling Emlyn Williams (president of the South Wales miners) that he disturbed me.

"And of course the South Wales executive almost to a man agreed with me. But then they said, 'He's the only one we've got, see, boy. The Left has decided.'"

Perhaps because of his political certainties, Scargill became one of the most effective mob orators of his time, all the more so because he didn't waste too much effort on logical argument or detailed analysis of his own or his opponents' case. Instead he articulated simple assertions with revivalist zeal and swept his audience along on the tide. His speech to the Labour Party conference in the autumn of 1984, in the middle of the strike, was breathtaking even by those standards.

"There are no uneconomic pits," he told an audience that had cheered and whistled in delirious approval as he'd made his way to the rostrum. "There are only pits which have been deliberately starved of investment by successive governments. If that investment

---

* Grunwick was a photographic processing factory in North West London that was the subject of a long and acrimonious industrial dispute in 1976-77. The company sacked Asian workers for joining a trade union. In the summer of 1977 a mass picket was staged and ended in a battle with the police. This was an incident that probably influenced the thinking of both Thatcher and Scargill. Supporters of action against the firm included members of the Labour cabinet who liked to pop along to be photographed on the picket line. Those who did so included Shirley Williams, later one of the founders of the SDP and, later still, the Liberal Democrat leader in the House of Lords.

had been put in those pits would still have been viable, producing valuable coal for the British people."

He was contemptuous about the nit-picking arguments put forward by people like the National Coal Board Chairman, Ian MacGregor, who talked the obscene language of capitalism, full of words like profit and loss and markets and selling. Scargill even imitated MacGregor's Scottish-American accent as he told delegates: "MacGregor says, 'Mr Scargill, what can we do with the coal?' I'll tell him what we can do with the millions of tons we produce. We can begin to practise compassion and give it to the old age pensioners in the twilight of their lives, that's what we can do with the coal on our ground."

It was a novel idea, employing miners to produce free coal for pensioners, a group that might even have included MacGregor, who was in his seventies. It didn't make any kind of sense, of course, but that was beside the point. This was ideological warfare and like everyone else the elderly had to be pressed into service of some kind. The audience cheered even louder than before.

The language of the conference hall is necessarily simplistic. It's the place (or, at least, it *was* the place) where politicians seek to convert and inspire at least as much as they want to persuade through the detailed logic of their case. The difference with Scargill, it turned out, was that he meant this stuff literally. He really believed that he could keep open every mine in Britain in which a ton or two of coal could still be discovered in some half-forgotten seam. But to do so, the implication was, he would have to defeat the government, and probably destroy it.

Scargill's critics, of whom there are a large number, insist that defeating the government was in fact the primary purpose of the whole dispute. He sought a confrontation, they say, in order to achieve the overthrow of a democratically elected government. Indeed, even some sympathisers believe that was the case. Tyrone O'Sullivan, lodge secretary at Tower Colliery, Hirwaun, during the strike, was a passionate supporter of Scargill's strategy then, although not of his subsequent career. He says without hesitation that Scargill had a political end in mind.

"Of course he did. Arthur does. Miners believe that. Miners don't want Tory governments. Miners have never wanted Tory governments. If the outcome of a battle with the miners is that there's no longer a Tory government I would say that's having your

Christmas twice. Winning the strike and then getting rid of the
bloody Tories. Of course it's political. When hasn't it been political
in the last hundred and fifty years?"

Which is not quite the same as saying that Scargill was bent on
revolution, a view held by many members of the government,
including the Secretary of State for Energy, Peter Walker. "When I
first took on the task I studied Scargill. And I read every leaflet he'd
ever written. I read all the cuttings for years back and all the speeches
he had made. And if you do that you realise there is an extreme dedicated Marxist at work. It was someone pursuing a political purpose
which, in my view, the majority of miners don't hold."

Well, yes, but throughout its history the NUM had been
packed to the roof with people you could describe as dedicated
Marxists – Arthur Horner, Will Paynter and Lawrence Daly as
successive general secretaries, for example, not to mention
Scargill's long-serving vice president, Mick McGahey. In all the
years they'd held positions of great authority they had failed to
advance the date of the arrival of the socialist millennium by a
single day. The difference now was that Scargill was leading the
union in a dispute with someone equally certain of her philosophy.
This wasn't a battle of Arthur's choosing, apologists argue, but of
Mrs Thatcher's. Nor did she stumble into it, they insist. She set
out, they say, with the deliberate intention of changing the British
industrial and political landscape.

Tony Benn makes this case in that famous everyone-knows-
this-is-true-so-there's-nothing-to-argue-about manner which has
drawn him so many admirers who look upon him as a toff turned
cuddly leftie who "talks a lot of sense, you know".

He says: "Mrs Thatcher decided, when she came to power, to
destroy British trade unionism. That was what it was about. It was
a counter-revolution… Mrs Thatcher decided to destroy trade
unionism and local government and indeed blank out democracy.
Mrs Thatcher decided that the power of the state would be put at
the disposal of capital against labour."

There are plenty other people who, although they don't in
general take the Benn view of political life, believe this to be more
or less the case. Certainly that Mrs Thatcher had decided to assert
the authority of government against the anarchic forces she associated with trade unionism in general, with the National Union of
Mineworkers heading the list of public enemies.

In these circumstances it's by no means far-fetched to look on what happened during the year of the miners' strike as the outcome of a confrontation between two people who were unswervingly convinced of the values of their political causes and traditions. And, even more dangerously, of their moral authority. Both of them maintained they were fighting for freedom, defining that idea in their own terms. It wasn't as simple as that, it never is, but nevertheless in March 1984 Britain embarked on what now looks like the last of the conflicts that had convulsed the country for generations. Unions against governments; workers against owners; socialism against capitalism. It was, too, the end of a certain kind of history.

*

A few days before he died in the summer of 2003, I went to visit Philip Weekes in hospital. He was suffering from leukaemia and, a few days before, he had been in a coma. He was eighty-three years old. He reached up from his bed and we shook hands. It was good of me to come, he said, in the rich accent of Nantybwch in the Monmouthshire valleys, a voice deepened still further by a life-time's consumption of approximately one million cigarettes. Then he then told me, entirely lucidly, a joke that had appealed to him that day. For the record, it was about Eamonn Casey, the Catholic Bishop of Galway who'd disappeared from Ireland when it became public that he'd had a son by his American mistress. He took refuge, the story went, in the Philippines, where he sought out the Archbishop of Manila, Cardinal Jaime Sin, so that he could make his confession. Thus, kneeling before the cardinal, the Bishop said: "Bless me, Sin, for I have fathered".

Some people, I suppose, maintain their singular character and their expression of it in pretty well all circumstances, as Philip Weekes did on that Saturday afternoon. I'd always known him as gregarious, tolerant, enthusiastic and adventurous, with a well-developed sense of mischief and a keen interest in the follies of the famous and the influential, not excluding some of his own colleagues in the higher reaches of the National Coal Board. So perhaps it wasn't surprising that he behaved towards me at the very end as he had done throughout the thirty years I had known him as a friend and as a substantial figure in Welsh public life, of which, from time to time, he helped me try and make journalistic sense.

Then there was the courage, too. I told this story of our last meeting to someone who had worked with him for a long time. "Ah well," he said, "he wouldn't have wanted people to see him *in extremis*." It was a resolution he brought to his public and private lives, sometimes in the most challenging circumstances.

He did so with style and good humour and even more valuably, a sense of proportion. Unusually among public men he even enjoyed his own *faux pas*. As the area director of the South Wales coalfield during one of the most turbulent periods of its troubled history he was embroiled in constant disputes over pit closures. In 1983 a stay-down strike was organised in an attempt to save a colliery where, a month earlier, he'd been greeted underground with a chalked message saying, as he recorded later, "Welcome Phil. Close the fucking place."

During the dispute he was challenged by an ITN interviewer who said closure would mean making 600 men redundant in the Rhondda Valley. He later wrote that, as he launched himself on his answer, he knew what he was going to say, but couldn't stop himself. "'Nonsense,' I said. 'Every man in that colliery will be offered a job within striking distance of his home.'"

He reflected later: "At least I got a mention in *The Listener* the following week under the heading of 'Sayings of the Week'."

This is one of the engagingly self-deprecating stories he noted about himself in a diary he kept intermittently for many years. It's a journal that reveals, too, his fierce commitment to the coal industry and his fury at the forces that seemed bent on bringing it down by accident or design; including some of the most senior figures in the NCB whose most cherished aim sometimes seemed to be, according to Philip, that anything bad that had to happen should happen, whenever possible, in South Wales.

In January 1981 he was writing: "I am more and more convinced that there's a plot afoot to get me, and consequently South Wales, to accept more than the seven closures I have already accepted for 1981/82 – AND I AM NOT GOING TO HAVE IT."

This is not, it quickly becomes clear, paranoia. Of course we have to make due allowances for partisanship, and Philip was invariably a passionate advocate of the interests of Wales. But what his diary gives us is an insider's account of the events that were eventually to destroy the British coal industry. He was at the heart of affairs not only as the South Wales area director, but also as a part-time member of the board itself from 1977 until 1984, by which time the last great strike was under way.

What emerges from Philip's diary is not a picture of a group of people including the NCB, the cabinet and senior civil servants, conducting a calculated campaign designed to crush the ambitions of Arthur Scargill and the National Union of Mineworkers. Quite the reverse, indeed, with the NCB leading the way in a staggering display of ineptitude, conspiracy, disloyalty and personal feuding that was operatic in its intensity. Once again, as you look behind the backdrop against which public life is played out on television and in the newspapers, you realise that far from the levers of power being operated in response to the visions of great people with powerful and tireless minds, they are more often than not pushed this way and that by the vagaries of the climate and quirks of personality.

If it was bad enough when the old guard were in charge, it degenerated to the point of black comedy with the arrival as Chairman on September 1, 1983, of Ian MacGregor, newly released from his task as the scourge of the British Steel Corporation. Brought up in Scotland and trained as a metallurgist, he had spent most of his working life in the United States in both the coal and steel industries. He was three weeks short of his seventy-first birthday.

Here was a third person who was to be play a central role in the events that were to unfold. Philip Weekes came to despise MacGregor, but he wasn't alone. So too did his boss, the Energy Secretary, Peter Walker, who wanted someone else entirely and made no secret of the fact that he thought MacGregor was useless. Their personal animosity was such that it continued long after the shutters had come down on the industry as they went on sniping at each other from the shelter of their respective autobiographies, books in which each man attempted to demonstrate how he'd been right about practically everything all along.

MacGregor wrote that, in June 1984, Mrs Thatcher made it clear that she had total confidence in him, although if you read even his own account carefully you suspect that might not have been a totally accurate reflection of her feelings. He was certainly to discover later that year that her mood could switch quickly enough to one of chilly disappointment. In fact doubts about his suitability seem to have bothered her quite early on. In a telling phrase she was later to say that MacGregor was "strangely lacking in guile". Sensitivity, too, one suspects, as MacGregor continued in his autobiography: "I don't know if her confidence in me was shared by Peter Walker. I suspect not. He always seemed to be much more concerned about political 'appearances' than she did and therefore expressed far greater anxieties than her – and did so more publicly."

Anyone with even a passing knowledge of Walker's career would recognise him from that description and no doubt MacGregor's incompetence when it came to public relations reinforced Walker's view that he was completely unsuitable for the job. But they couldn't get rid of him either, since Scargill would have claimed it as a victory. "Few things would please him more," Walker wrote, continuing dismissively, "What we had to do was to ensure that Mr MacGregor remained tolerably cheerful." This was not the kind of personal chemistry that was likely to be very helpful in presenting the necessary image of solidarity of purpose between the government and the coal board. And when we remember, too, that these exchanges took place at second-hand between grown-ups long after the events described, we realise that public life isn't invariably conducted at the elevated level innocent voters might otherwise assume.

In these circumstances, though, you might ask whether the appointment of MacGregor was in fact a stroke of political genius by Mrs Thatcher. Admittedly there were times when, as the strike proceeded, she certainly didn't think so, and by the end she'd lost her admiration for the old man. MacGregor lacked one indispensable talent for this rough game. He had no sense of political touch and on two separate occasions almost wrecked the whole enterprise. Even so, by appointing him in the first place it might have crossed Mrs Thatcher's mind that she would combine two objectives. The first was to intimidate and anger the NUM because of MacGregor's record. At British Steel he'd faced down a thirteen-week strike and had then proceeded to slash the workforce. The clear message was that he'd bring the same sort of methods to the coal industry. Certainly MacGregor didn't seem to make much of an effort to woo his new employees. He talked the language of international business and told colliers in Yorkshire that women miners in the United States could work harder than they did. There was nothing more inflammatory in the British coalfields than that kind of talk. There's certainly good reason to believe that his appointment helped to accelerate a further move to the left in elections to the NUM's National Executive.

By May of the following year Philip Weekes, in a secret meeting with Emlyn Williams and George Rees, the South Wales miners' General Secretary, was making an unusual request. He wanted to persuade MacGregor to direct some capital investment to the South Wales coalfield. He was well advanced in his long-running campaign to get a new mine opened at Margam. Meanwhile he had a request for the injection of a modest element of diplomacy into matters. Would they please stop referring to MacGregor in public as "a geriatric American butcher".

They agreed.

Mrs Thatcher's second objective in appointing MacGregor was to put a stop to the feebleness and complacency she could see all around her. She wanted to break the old, inclusive nature of the coal board and the special relationships between management and the unions. They had a long history of dispute, including two national strikes in the seventies, but they still had more in common with each other than they had with anyone else. MacGregor didn't speak the same language. But then, neither did Scargill.

In her autobiography Mrs Thatcher was savagely critical about the way in which the industry had operated until that time. McGregor, she thought, was just the man to put a stop to the feebleness and complacency she could see all about her. Even in retrospect her language is inflammatory.

"Within the NCB he [Ian MacGregor] found himself surrounded by people who had made their careers in an atmosphere of appeasement and collaboration with the NUM and who greatly resented the changed atmosphere he brought with him."

Appeasement and collaboration, eh? Two of the dirtiest words in the political war vocabulary. If she thought that when reflecting in comparative tranquillity years later, what, you wonder, did she think at the time? Looking back now you can see that such an explosive mixture of personality and political and economic philosophy was being assembled that a firestorm of some kind could hardly be avoided. But was there a deliberate strategy in which MacGregor and Scargill, being the kind of people they were, would inevitably come to the decisive show-down the government desired? You didn't have to tell them specifically what to do, they'd do it anyway, they couldn't help themselves, even if resolution on the MacGregor side needed a little stiffening from time to time.

Throughout the strike the government went round trying to pretend the whole affair wasn't really anything to do with them, a stratagem that fooled nobody. They were about as convincing as a delinquent schoolboy leaving the scene whistling, with his hands in his pockets; Billy Bunter denying a crime before he'd been told that it had actually taken place. "I didn't take your cake, Cherry."

But then, officially keeping a distance was second nature to a government which was understandably nervous of the miners and their grip on public admiration and support. So the Weekes diaries report an event in May 1983 when the NCB nationally had just agreed to the closure of Brynlliw Colliery at Gorseinon, west of Swansea, which was losing up to six million pounds a year. The announcement was to be made on May 16 but then Mrs Thatcher named the election date: it was to be June 9.

"On Monday evening Jimmy Cowan (the NCB Deputy Chairman) telephoned me at home. He and Norman (Siddall, the NCB Chairman) had just returned from a meeting with Nigel Lawson, our true blue, straight-shootin' Secretary of State for Energy. Lawson had asked, instructed, that we delay the announcement on Brynlliw until after the election! I was very angry – but not of course with Jimmy. Indeed, I could hardly believe my ears, because although I knew that they would cut and run at some time this year, I never expected it so soon.

"Anyhow, I conformed with HMG's wish, secretly with malicious glee, and cancelled Monday's Brynlliw meeting because of 'unexpected urgent business'.

"I shall take a day off."

★

The more you look at it, the more the idea of Mrs Thatcher having some kind of master plan to destroy the NUM and consequently to emasculate the rest of the trade union movement seems extravagantly far-fetched. Indeed, the idea of any government not only having a master plan but actually managing to carry it out is contradicted by everything we know about political life. There is no better example of that than the hapless and blighted journey undertaken by the Heath government. What Mrs Thatcher clearly

did take from that experience, what joined the strike of 1974 with
that of 1984, was one simple idea: the Government must not lose.
She spelt out the principle in her autobiography: "The fall of Ted
Heath's Government after a General Election precipitated by the
1973-74 miners' strike lent substance to the myth that the NUM
had the power to make or break British Governments, or at least
veto any policy threatening their interests by preventing coal
getting to the power stations."

Even old Labour governments might have subscribed to that
point of view (in private at least) but no Labour government ever
had to confront an official national strike by the NUM, something
else that underlined the idea that there was a traditional political
struggle going on in the eighties. Not losing in a strike, and, even
more important, not being seen to lose in a strike, was the objective of every administration. But apart from that aim it's difficult
to see much evidence of there being a brilliantly orchestrated plan
to lure the miners to their doom.

That doesn't mean there is no evidence at all, but much of the
conduct of that strike was on all sides a total shambles. There was
certainly one occasion when Arthur Scargill might have walked
away with a reputation as an outstanding tactician, someone who
had maintained the reputation of the NUM as an organisation to
be feared and placated. There was another when, months into the
strike, the government and the coal board, thanks to Ian
MacGregor, nearly manoeuvred themselves to defeat. If the NUM
in general, and Scargill in particular, had not been so obsessed
with a mistaken and inflated view of their own history there might
have been a different outcome. If they'd thought more deeply they
might simply have looked at the clear evidence that the government
had taken on board the basic lesson of 1972 and 1974 and was
acting accordingly. That evidence could be most clearly seen, paradoxically, in a decision by the government to give in to the miners.

It happened early in 1981, when Joe Gormley was still the
union's president. The coal board, with the support of the Energy
Secretary, David Howell, put forward plans to close 23 pits with the
loss of 13,000 jobs. Cuts on this scale seemed certain to provoke a
strike. Gormley threatened one, but in South Wales, where five
collieries were due to be closed, they simply got on with it. Men at
one pit walked out within a couple of days of hearing the news.
Then, on February 17, a coalfield conference decided on a total

strike. It looked as though a Conservative government would again be locked in a long and damaging conflict with the NUM.

However, the next day, on the evening of February 18, arriving home after making the necessary arrangements to cope with the strike in South Wales, Philip Weekes rang his elderly mother.

"To my amazement she told me there'd been a newsflash on TV which alleged that the NCB had withdrawn their closure plan. I was convinced that she'd got it all wrong until I heard the eight pm radio news – and sure enough she was right. Having heard subsequent news bulletins, it appears that the Cabinet had given sloppy David Howell instructions to execute – not a U-turn – but a somersault. I can still hardly believe it."

In fact David Howell had received his instructions directly from the Prime Minister herself. Later she wrote: "I was appalled to find that we had inadvertently entered into a battle which we could not win. There had been no forward thinking in the Department of Energy about what would happen in the case of a strike: it was the stocks at the power stations which were important and these were simply not sufficient. I had by now even less confidence in the NCB management. It became clear that all we could do was cut our losses and live to fight another day when – with adequate preparation – we might be in a position to win."

It's clear that Mrs Thatcher had learnt from the disasters of the seventies, as she was to learn still further from this debacle, but the NUM, used to pushing Tory governments about, almost certainly misunderstood the significance of the 1981 withdrawal. On the face of it, it looked like an abject surrender by a nervous government, but in reality it was the action of people who understood that, if there was to be a confrontation, the ground had to be chosen very carefully.

Phoning around political and industrial contacts the day after the climbdown, Philip Weekes pieced together a picture of what had happened at the meeting between the coal board, the unions and the Department of Energy.

"In the meeting at five o clock, Howell had spoken from a prepared statement, but when the unions and the board – in particular Gormley – had said their pieces, he cast down his eyes and became rather bumbling and confused. What, after all, can you expect of an Energy Minister who spent his formative years in Eton and the Guards?"

Howell said the government was willing to talk about a different approach. The Weekes diaries go on: "Joe leapt in and praised Howell and the Government for its common sense and courage in performing the largest and quickest U-turn ever and turned to Derek (Ezra) to make his contribution by lifting the closure threat.

"Derek looked at Howell questioningly and, according to one source, at that moment a fly landed on the Secretary of State's ear and he twitched. Derek thought he had nodded vigorously and so he volunteered 'in the circumstances' to withdraw the threat."

A lot of people, and I admit to being among them, were persuaded by that event to believe that the government still walked in fear of the NUM. What we know now is that this was a sign of its strength rather than weakness. If the NUM wanted a fight it wouldn't take place until Mrs Thatcher and her ministers were ready.

Joe Gormley seems not to have grasped what was going on. He rushed from the meeting to explain to the television cameras the extent of what he presented as his personal triumph. Later, in his autobiography, he presented it all over again.

"Whether Maggie Thatcher knew what her climbdown would cost, I have no idea... But I wasn't crowing. I didn't regard it as a victory for the miners, as such, but for the industry and for Britain, and for commonsense.

"After that first meeting with Howell, the *Observer* quoted a coal board official as having admired what I did at the meeting, and saying: 'Joe could bargain the buttons off their trousers'. Well, I'm not sure I wanted that! But I wouldn't ask for a much better summary of anything I've been able to achieve.

"Negotiating has been my life."

Now, of course, we understand that stand-off much better than Joe Gormley did at the time. It looked as though the coal industry was continuing on traditional lines, even if the tradition wasn't actually as much as a decade old. The NCB and the NUM would sort it out between them and inform the government of their decisions later. But it wasn't the same and Gormley didn't get it. When Mrs Thatcher made Peter Walker Energy Secretary after the 1983 election he saw that her attitude to the miners had been hardened by the experience.

Walker wrote later: "She was properly nervous of the harm a miners' dispute could do to the economy. She had been with me in Ted Heath's Cabinet in 1974 and seen the damage done then.

But the 1981 humiliation when she was Prime Minister was clearly scorched on her mind."

In one sense Mrs Thatcher was perhaps all the more dangerous because she was isolated from, and entirely unsympathetic to, the intricate relationships within the mining industry in which both management and the NUM were often equally unimpressed by government efforts to be decisive. After the 1981 deal, Philip Weekes noted Gormley's arrival at a meeting at the coal board several days later.

"During the buffet lunch while [Norman] Siddall [then the NCB Deputy Chairman] and I were talking, in strutted Joe with his hat on and trying to look like his public image in the Tory press. He waddled straight up to us, grinned, winked and said, 'Well, Phil, 'ow are them fuckers in South Wales?'

"This immediately set my teeth on edge because I know he assumed all South Wales miners are lazy and Communist and completely in tune with their local leaders.

"I made a cold and probably sarcastic reply and Gormley, nudging Siddall and winking and grinning at the same time, said: 'I always knew it was a mistake to put a strong Welshman to run the coalfield. He and the men speak the same language.' Gormley loathes the Welsh miners and he believes that if they worked harder all our problems would be solved."

This encounter shows very clearly the complex culture that characterised the nationalised coal industry. The traditional antagonisms between management and unions were only a part of it. Regional and political alliances were just as important – Gormley's Lancashire Labour distrust of the South Wales Left, also substantially Labour but to Gormley the wrong sort of Labour and with a long Communist tradition behind that, being just one example. The Weekes diaries illustrate just how convoluted were the considerations that influenced decisions made within the NCB. As far as he was concerned they were instrumental in attempts to manoeuvre South Wales into taking more than its fair share of closures.

"Part of this devious affair is Joe Gormley's natural desire not to offend the moderate executive members on the N West and the N East, and his dislike of Emlyn Williams and George Rees. [The South Wales members of the NUM executive.] He is encouraged, I would imagine, by Norman Siddall whose great weekend chum is Ray Hunter – another Yorkshire man who runs the Western area, including

Lancashire. Hunter has rattled sabres for years about the need to close uneconomic pits and about the Chairman's lack of resolution."

At this distance just a flavour of the labyrinthine conspiracies of the industry is all that is necessary to show that it occupied a place that, partly because of the nature of mining, physically remote from most people's experience, largely excluded the rest of the world. Union officials conspired with senior managers to get the better of other union officials. Members of the board conspired against each other with the help of whoever was to hand. And to some extent they all conspired against the then Chairman, Derek Ezra, because he was an accountant and therefore to them not a part of the real brotherhood. At the same time, though, Joe Gormley also conspired with Ezra. It was to Philip Weekes's fury, for example, in 1981, that the two men privately agreed to keep open Deep Duffryn colliery, near Mountain Ash, which Philip wanted to close. Philip was so cross that he immediately went out and replaced his old Rover with a new Jaguar, bought at the board's expense. Much more damagingly for the NUM, but to the advantage of the coal board and the government, Gormley and Ezra had also come to a deal to introduce a productivity scheme in the industry. It turned the clock back on the unified wages system that had brought a brief and fragile unity of purpose to the disparate British coalfields. It was on that unity that the successful strikes of 1972 and 1974 were founded. By 1984 it no longer existed.

In fact the whole corporate culture, often malicious and devious, was about to be obliterated by three people who refused to subscribe to it. Margaret Thatcher despised it, perhaps the one thing she had in common with Arthur Scargill. Ian MacGregor seems to have been baffled by it, as he was by a number of things but, since he had been chosen specifically to put the bulldozers through it, that perhaps didn't matter very much. But it's also in MacGregor's part in this whole affair that we get some genuine ambiguity about the designs of the coal board (and so of the government, at second hand) when it came to confronting the NUM. One interpretation is that MacGregor wanted a fight and went out of his way to provoke it. Anticipating the philosophy of George W. Bush it certainly looked as though he was doing it to them before they did it to him.

MacGregor was fond of using the phrases of western movies. He sometimes talked in terms of a shootout at noon. "Let's get the

wagons in a circle, Phil," he once said to a baffled Philip Weekes.
And here we were in a sense on the verge of that last encounter at
the OK Corral in which the forces of law and order, often including many flawed people, reluctantly prepare to confront the
desperadoes who threaten a fragile community. In the end a
government's got to do what a government's got to do, the argument goes, and it's got to do it with the modern state equivalent of
a six gun and a rifle. There's no point in wearing a marshal's badge
if you don't understand what it demands of you.

MacGregor himself put it in similarly melodramatic terms.
"On the day I joined the National Coal Board, 1 September 1983,
Arthur Scargill had already decided to have his strike. All that
remained to be settled was the date. And I was already determined,
with the support of the Prime Minister, that I was going to have as
much say as possible in the selection of that day."

It's important to be cautious when examining such statements,
of course, since it comes from MacGregor's autobiography, a form
of literature that often occupies that marshy ground somewhere
between fact and romantic fiction. And the person who wrote that
paragraph (presumably Rodney Tyler, MacGregor's collaborator on
the book) obviously wanted this part of the story to be as journalis-
tically eye-catching as possible. But there were others who thought
that perhaps there had been a deliberate attempt to provoke Scargill
and the NUM. Among them was Philip Weekes. In May, more than
two months after the strike started, he reflected on its origins.

He noted that there was an over-estimate of the extent to
which the board would need to cut capacity. What MacGregor had
done was to compare the estimates of production for 1984-85
with the estimates for the previous year. The point was that the
actual production figures for 1983-84 were considerable lower
than the estimates. The real cut would therefore be substantially
less than that implied in MacGregor's statement. Philip says that
presumably this was done deliberately. In other words MacGregor
reversed normal management practice by inflating the threat to
jobs in the industry. Surely he must have seen how inflammatory
that would be. "The final provocation," Philip Weekes goes on,
"was to declare Cortonwood Colliery closed."

Cortonwood was in South Yorkshire, the heart of Scargill
country and closing it was bound to provoke a fierce reaction from
the NUM president. Philip's account says that the closure was

Out! Out! Out! >>   55

ordered by the NCB Deputy Chairman, Jimmy Cowan ("the
board's worst communicator") who hadn't actually told the people
most intimately concerned, including the Yorkshire area director,
George Hayes. The closure review procedures appeared not to
have been adhered to and the news had come as a total surprise to
the unions, all the more so because more men had actually been
signed on at the pit a few weeks earlier.

"In the strike that followed," says Weekes, "which has affected
three quarters of the Board's activities, the two main protagonists
– Scargill and MacGregor – have, by their public statements, made
the issue almost a personal contest. Scargill, of course, grabbed the
large pieces of bait that MacGregor, presumably with HMG's full
knowledge and support, had thrown him. He couldn't very well
have missed it, but he swallowed it as if it had been the one thing
he'd been waiting for."

It's here that we come to the most remarkable aspect of this
whole affair, the unique proposition that singled it out from all the
great mining disputes of history. The strikes of 1972 and 1974 had
been about pay and conditions. So had the events of 1926,
although that was not a campaign for more money but an effort to
stop the owners paying less. One of the most famous mining
conflicts of all, which led to the Tonypandy riots in 1910, was
about pay rates. This time, though, it was different. How much
miners got paid had nothing to do with it. In a sense, as even some
of his opponents say to this day, Arthur was right: this was essentially a struggle for the very existence of the British coal industry.

This was an extraordinary break in industrial policy, not least
for the miners themselves. They were used to opposing the
closures of individual pits, occasionally with temporary successes,
but they had never adopted the idea that the industry was something to be saved for future generations. Quite the reverse, indeed,
since one of the great traditions of mining was to maintain that it
was a rotten job and the sooner all the pits were closed the better.
Not until there were other, more congenial, occupations perhaps,
but as a principle it was entirely rational. Mining is perhaps the
most reviled industry in the entire world. It has been the cause of
injury, illness and premature death for hundreds of thousands,
perhaps millions of people.

Yet in 1984 the case was being put forward by the NUM, led
by an unstoppably passionate Scargill, that this state of affairs

should be maintained at any cost. That, regardless of any economic considerations or, indeed, regardless of any idea that there might actually be a better way for the people concerned to live and work, pits should be kept open until the last grains of anything recognisable as coal had been wound to the surface. In the autumn of 1984 Scargill spelt this out to a Labour Party conference that roared its endorsement of his economic and social analysis.

"I'm sick and tired of the balance sheet mentality of this government and the coal board, talking about the fact that people will not be made compulsorily redundant. I want to make it clear to this conference, we're not talking about a miner in work whose job may be made redundant. It's not his job to sell. It belongs to future generations. And all our movement should go on record in support of that principle and policy."

If this was an argument that one of the compelling reasons for having a mining industry was to provide employment for miners and, in due course, for miners' sons, delegates didn't pause to consider its implications. They just went on cheering and applauding. Of course they knew it was unsustainable, but the sheer brilliance of Scargill's oratory and the emotional grip of the mining tradition carried them beyond any considerations of logic.

For the moment they didn't ask why the miners should be different. Why, for instance, they should avoid the fate of the London dockers who, like the miners, had fought with vigour and ingenuity and some success against the Heath government in the seventies, but who had nevertheless in the end been overwhelmed and their jobs obliterated. Or, closer to home in places like Wales, the steelworkers who, at the beginning of the eighties, had struck for three months over pay, claimed an ambiguous victory and then been confronted by Ian MacGregor, brought into the British Steel Corporation to turn the industry upside down and shake out thousands of jobs. And what were these same steelworkers to make of Arthur Scargill who wanted them to save his members' jobs with their own? That at least was the implication of his attempt to cut off coal supplies to the steelworks, the consequences of which could have been the permanent closure of some of those works and the loss of all future employment in them. What would have followed from that would have been a further reduction in the market for coal. But, hey, who cares about markets? Give it to the pensioners.

What remains most puzzling about Scargill, though, is the

timing of the strike. It began at the end of the winter, when the demand for coal and other forms of energy was going into a seasonal decline. The government, preparing for a confrontation, had deliberately built up coal stocks and invested heavily in other forms of power generation. In these circumstances a strike was clearly not going to have the public impact of the previous disputes when the lights went out, industry went on to a three day week and shops ran out of candles. In any case, Mrs Thatcher's industrial relations legislation, a much more robust piece of fire-fighting equipment than that devised by the Heath government, curtailed the prospects of other unions being able to offer useful, practical support. A strike in these circumstances seems crazy now and it seemed crazy then. Perhaps the government was indeed smart enough to put him a position where he could only do what they wanted him to do, call a strike when they held all the advantages. But even if this were true they surely couldn't have guessed the self-immolating lengths to which he would take it.

In the end it was perhaps Scargill's imperfect understanding of history, his groundless optimism that some kind of workers' uprising would drive a Conservative government from office, his inept strategy and his intransigence in negotiations, that prevented the NUM from saving anything from this grim affair except, at the last moment, a certain amount of dignity. But it was also the case, we can now see, that there was an inevitability about this strike that went far beyond Scargill's powers of leadership. Indeed you can argue that it had to happen because no one knew what else to do.

Twenty years later, riding navy-suited through London in the back of his government Rover, Kim Howells still struggled to reconcile what he did in 1984 with what he came to believe later. Like others who were at the heart of the dispute he wrestled with the idea that the miners charged to certain defeat because their history and character would not allow them to do otherwise. "Were we wrong?" Kim wondered. "I don't know. It's the old problem of did we have any alternative?"

Terry Thomas, in 1984 the South Wales miners' vice president, still believes there was no real choice. A failed strike would in many ways have been no worse than a decision simply to watch as the government and the coal board dismantled a huge section of the industry. "I am honestly of the opinion that the strike would have taken place irrespective of who the national leaders of the NUM

were, whether Joe Gormley had still been there, whether it had been
Arthur Scargill. (The government's policy of reducing coal production)... meant inevitably there were vast numbers of jobs in the
mining industry going to be destroyed. That gauntlet being thrown
down by the coal board would have been picked up by the miners.
I think the pressure on the leadership would have been such that the
strike would have taken place irrespective of the leadership."

What you get from such conversations is a sense that there was
some kind of emotional need among many miners to make a last
stand for the survival of their industry. It wasn't a matter of practical calculation, but a demonstration of defiance that might not
have stood the test of the self-questioning that would have been
provoked by a ballot on the issue.

"There is no doubt in my mind," Terry Thomas said, "that if
there had been a ballot there would have been no strike. In South
Wales it wasn't that they didn't believe in the cause, that's not what
their doubts were about. Their doubts were about whether we could
win. And how long we would have to stay out on strike to win."

These two ideas, which are of course mutually unsustainable,
are at the core of the paradox that was to wreck the National
Union of Mineworkers and the British coal industry. A ballot
might well have meant no strike. Not having a ballot undermined
the legitimacy of the action in the public eye and split the union
for ever. Under threat, the only weapon the miners had available
was that of a national strike; but at the same time there was clearly
a recognition that striking was almost certainly the wrong thing to
do. So much so that even the South Wales miners, whose militancy
had long been a matter of legend, were deeply divided over the
action. The lodges voted by 18 to 13 against supporting the strike
that had begun in Yorkshire.

Kim Howells said: "I think the men knew, and we knew, that
there was very little chance of us winning. On that first weekend it
was quite clear that there was going to be a majority of NUM
lodges in the coalfield that were going to vote against taking strike
action. It threw everyone into a panic."

That panic wasn't about the need to support Yorkshire, where
it had all begun over Cortonwood, but an awareness that if some
collieries struck and others didn't, it would lead to bitterness and
violence in the coalfield as Welsh miners fought each other. As we
were to see soon enough, that would probably have been an

inevitable outcome. If there was to be a strike then it was essential that everyone should support it.

"Our greatest horror," Kim said, "was that we would find Yorkshire pickets coming into South Wales. That was seen as something we would subsequently be ashamed of. A group of us met at the ambulance room at Tower Colliery, near Hirwaun. We had a very good network through the coalfield of left wingers. We phoned everybody we knew and we had our first meeting on Sunday morning and our second meeting late on Sunday afternoon. By then we'd organised pickets to go to every pit in the coalfield. It took us till the following Thursday to get all the pits out on strike. It was completely unconstitutional."

The story of the sour and often violent year that followed is well known and it's easy enough to describe it now as some kind of deluded adventure which was always going to end in disaster. But even that need not have been true, thanks to the efforts of Ian MacGregor. As matters turned out any leader of the NUM other than Arthur Scargill would have paid good money to have MacGregor as his leading opponent. In a few months he seemed to have given up his role as a hired gunslinger, put on a long brown apron and adopted more homespun methods of speech.

In July there was a dock strike provoked by a dispute over the unloading of coal for the steelworks at Scunthorpe. MacGregor, who was about to begin the first peace talks with the NUM was sent for by a distinctly edgy Prime Minister. He wrote later that she "wished to be reassured that it was not really my intention to give away the store".

He gave the necessary reassurance, but if he wasn't planning to hand over the actual store he certainly offered most of its contents to the people on the other side of the table. Their only shortcoming as negotiators, it emerged, was that they didn't actually want to negotiate. The distance between the NUM and the coal board came down to one issue. Scargill insisted that no pit should be closed on economic grounds. Closure was to be accepted only if working conditions were unsafe or reserves were totally exhausted. The coal board side suggested something more flexible so that where a comprehensive investigation "shows that a colliery has no further mineable reserves that are workable and which can be beneficially developed, such a colliery shall be deemed exhausted".

By the standards of the fudge factory in which industrial

agreements are manufactured, this seemed to most people to be a perfectly serviceable model. There was plenty of scope for arguments on both sides about what words like 'mineable', 'workable' and 'beneficially' might mean, but the NUM could have presented this as a stupendous victory achieved by the selfless sacrifice of the British miners, apart, of course, from those scabs in the Midlands who might consequently find their lives a bit difficult. It wouldn't have stopped all closures but in the future the coal board would have to proceed very cautiously. That would have conformed to a long tradition of negotiation and settlement in which both sides emerge with something. Once more Scargill demonstrated his contempt for tradition and turned it down.

As it happened his reaction was enthusiastically welcomed in Downing Street where Mrs Thatcher had been looking on anxiously. She understood perfectly well the way in which the proposed form of words could have been represented as a triumph for the NUM.

She recalled: "There was a real danger that the talks would end by fudging the issue on the closure of uneconomic pits: a formula was being developed based upon the proposition that no pit should be closed if it was capable of being 'beneficially developed'. The NCB was also prepared to give a commitment to keep open five named pits that the NUM had claimed were due for closure. We were very alarmed. Not only were there ambiguities in the detailed wording of the proposals, but (far worse) a settlement on these lines would have given Mr Scargill the chance to claim victory.

"But on 18 July... negotiations collapsed. I have to say I was enormously relieved."

Well, apart from what many people would see as a missed opportunity for the NUM, the question arises once more in a different form – what if? MacGregor clearly had the power to reach a settlement and once the details had been agreed there could have been no going back, no matter how strongly Downing Street felt about it. In these circumstances one wonders again about the persistent belief that Mrs Thatcher's overarching aim was to destroy the NUM. Here was a moment when in fact the union's authority and its reputation as the scourge of Tory governments would simply have been reinforced. But it nearly happened and all she could have done would have been to fume impotently at the incompetence of others.

At this stage Mrs Thatcher must have been having increasing doubts about MacGregor. His reputation as a determined and unsentimental manager, unencumbered by the freemasonry that shaped the conduct of the industry, already seemed rather threadbare. But he had by no means finished with his efforts to see to it that the NUM must triumph after all. As Philip Weekes put it: "The Chairman succeeded in getting a second front launched!"

The National Association of Colliery Overmen, Deputies and Shotfirers represented supervisors in the coal industry who were responsible for mine safety. It was illegal to carry out mining work without the presence of NACODS members. They had never staged a national strike in their entire history and their edgy relationship with the NUM – echoing the traditional friction between foremen and the shop floor – meant they were disinclined to take action to support the miners' cause. Indeed, their presence was essential for the continued production of coal in the Midlands and the ability of the coal board to persuade more and more miners to return to work. Ian MacGregor somehow managed to get them to the stage where they voted by almost five to one in favour of a strike.

Their grievance was a simple one. In the early days of the strike, NACODS members who were confronted by NUM pickets were allowed to turn away from work and go home. In August they were instructed that where working miners were crossing picket line to go into their pits NACODS members would be expected to do so as well or they wouldn't be paid. NACODS responded by calling a strike ballot and, for good measure, demanding that the board's closure programme should be withdrawn.

Quite remarkably, MacGregor didn't think a NACODS strike would be much of a problem, as long as Nottingham could be kept working. The Energy Secretary, Peter Walker, was astonished at his attitude. McGregor wrote later: "… my view was met with a somewhat amazed response. I was asked in incredulous tones: 'You mean you're prepared to let them go on strike?' When I replied in the affirmative he, Walker, said: 'You must be out of your mind'."

It was at this point that the Prime Minister's admiration for MacGregor appears to have been finally extinguished. He was sent for "in very short order" and put his case to Mrs Thatcher. His memoirs reveal very clearly his failure to grasp what politics was all about. Mrs Thatcher spelt it out for him.

"The atmosphere in the Prime Minister's study on this occasion was very different from our earlier meeting. Clearly the enormous anxieties of her ministers had been passed on." (In the MacGregor version of life Mrs Thatcher is never worried herself, she is just made anxious by the concerns of lesser people.)

"I started to tell her that I thought we were beginning to see our way to a successful solution to the main dispute, and that I was confident that the NACODS dispute was not critically important. The Prime Minister cut in sharply. 'Well, I'm very worried about it. You have to realise the fate of this government is in your hands, Mr MacGregor. You have got to solve this problem.'"

At this point MacGregor (and his co-author) bring out the violins and the Mills and Boon handbook of romantic prose. "I felt the atmosphere between us had changed." How right he was. Rather earlier in fact, she'd raised with Walker the question of sacking MacGregor. Walker was all for it in principle but decided it would only encourage Scargill. But even as love was being withdrawn in that Downing Street study, MacGregor could think only that he was right and that the Prime Minister was somehow being got at by more feeble members of the cabinet.

"The impression I got was that she thought I was showing a cavalier disregard for the perils she and her government faced. It was clear that she must have been under great pressure from members of her cabinet including, I presumed, my immediate boss. I began to realise I was no longer talking to a Prime Minister who was free to make all the decisions and was confident of success. Her attitude as a master politician was, naturally, more coloured and sensitized by public opinion than mine. She was very concerned about maintaining the government's support. But she was also beginning to see a picture painted for her of defeat if NACODS came out on strike and it must have been painted for her very vividly indeed."

This is effortlessly brilliant comic writing – Mr Pooter as senior industrialist. What did he think prime ministers and governments spent their time thinking about other than their image and success and not looking as though they were blundering to defeat? Even worse, *actually* blundering to defeat. How could anyone think in positive terms about the decision of a trade union composed of moderate, conservative-minded men, to go on strike for the first time in their history? What if the working miners of

Nottinghamshire were unable to produce any more coal because there was no safety cover? In those circumstances Mr MacGregor and, much more important, the government, could justifiably have been accused of being unable to run a whelk stall.

Mrs Thatcher could hardly have been more explicit. Fix it, she told MacGregor and ("The good soldier always accepts the commander's orders…") fix it he did, not only rescinding the order that NACODS members should have to cross picket lines, but also by creating an independent review body on colliery closures. It was more fudge, but good enough for NACODS, who called off their strike. Perhaps, some people in the union thought, the NUM could claim this independent review body, of indeterminate authority, was just what they were looking for, climb on the back of it and, after seven months on strike, claim it as a great victory. Arthur Scargill simply said that the NACODS negotiators were "fools".

It's this catalogue of chance and error and misjudgement that seems to me to undermine the theory that for a decade and more Mrs Thatcher, to whom supernatural powers of malevolence are often attributed, brooded over a obsessive desire to wreak some kind of revenge on Britain's miners. If that had been the case then select-ing Ian MacGregor as her chosen instrument was a serious mistake.

As the dispute broke all known records for intransigence, punctuated by the refusal of the Scargill-led NUM to conform to the 'normal' practices and traditions of industrial relations, the government and the coal board might have moved towards to the point where their thoughts did actually turn to the idea of achiev-ing unconditional surrender. It might, though, have been something brought about as much by drift as by the adoption of a specific policy.

In October Philip Weekes was writing in his diary: "MacGregor's hold on the situation seems to have slipped gradu-ally in recent months and he has undoubtedly come under increasing pressure from No.10. The last two meetings that we've held with area directors and the few remaining full-time board members have brought out his inability to direct a meeting, or to sum up a discussion, then lay down the policy to be followed. Jimmy Cowan sits on his right, but he has a habit of burying his head in his hands and muttering celtic incantations. At both these meetings directors have either interrupted the Chairman or talked across the table without MacGregor doing anything to control them. He appears sometimes these days to be bemused or disinterested, or maybe he's wishing himself back in Florida."

For all his reputation as an axeman, this doesn't look to me like the kind of person you'd entrust with a contract to take out Arthur Scargill. It seems likely that Mrs Thatcher discovered that a bit late in the whole enterprise but even so, an elaborate and considered strategy? Surely not. Or perhaps not at the beginning. What is more than a possibility is that the idea of crushing the NUM and of wrecking the authority of Arthur Scargill did eventually become an official objective. Philip Weekes came to think so, with some reason.

In January 1985, many weary months into the dispute, talks got under way once more. They appeared to be making considerable progress when an article appeared in the *Evening Standard* saying they'd "broken down". They hadn't but, according to Philip, the story had been deliberately placed by NCB officials because the talks were proceeding too well. Further statements from the board laid preconditions on Scargill. "So," Philip wrote, "that killed that."

Among the objections to progress in the talks was that publicity about them had seriously affected the back to work movement. "It became increasingly apparent thereafter that Mrs T wanted Scargill's head on a platter and, in all probability, the destruction of the NUM, before negotiations would again be considered."

Later he was to write: "Everything I see and hear confirms my early view that the PM could not have done a greater disservice to Britain in every way when she appointed Ian K. MacGregor as Chairman of the NCB. I believe now that his, and maybe her, sole objectives were to smash Scargill and reduce once and for all the power of the NUM and maybe, too, set up the British coal mining industry for dismemberment. By those criteria he has done a remarkable job."

Now we know that's pretty much what did happen. Perhaps it would have happened anyway without a year-long strike and the wounds it opened up between individuals and within communities. One reason it was both symbolically and practically important was, as I've said, because it was the last great battle between organised labour and a British government. It seems unlikely that such a thing could ever happen again in that form. It was a fence erected between a long industrial and political history and an entirely different kind of world.

There was probably no group of workers more aware of that

history than the miners. Grievances were carried down the years like family feuds. The events of the seventies and the eighties were specifically announced by the miners themselves to have their origins at least as far back as 1926 and the General Strike in which wounds were inflicted on them by owners, the government and, most cruelly of all in their view, by other unions. In at least one speech in 1984 Arthur Scargill called up that memory when he said that, for the first time since 1926, soup kitchens had been set up in Britain's coalfields.

It's almost uncanny how the grudges of 1926 emerged again, almost undiluted, in 1984. Words written a matter of months after the General Strike applied almost exactly more than half a century later. "If we were deserted and left to fight a lone fight it was not by the workers that we were abandoned. Their hearts beat true to the end. From the workers of our country, and of the world, especially from the Trade Unionists of Russia, we obtained unstinted aid. For the help given, whether from Union funds or from individual workers, we convey the gratitude of miners' wives and children."

That quotation is taken from a statement made by the Miners' Federation of Great Britain to a TUC conference in January 1927. Behind those words of gratitude for international working class solidarity there is a burning resentment of the role of the TUC. The General Council called the General Strike at one minute to midnight on May 3,1926, in support of the miners, only to abandon it nine days later. It wasn't until the following December that the miners themselves were forced to return to work with their campaign against cuts in their wages unfulfilled. When they wrote, "If we were deserted and left to fight a lone fight..." they meant deserted by the TUC, something that was to have a direct influence on the conduct of the strikes in the seventies and the eighties.

Another observation might also have been carried unaltered across the years. "The sign of the weakness of our position at that time was the break in the Nottingham coalfield. In other areas, although men were going back to work in small numbers, the strike, broadly speaking, was solid."

That comes from the autobiography of Arthur Horner, the Merthyr Communist who had become President of the South Wales Miners' Federation in 1936 and General Secretary of the NUM in 1946. In 1984 it was again to be the men in the Midlands coalfields, notably those in Nottingham, who were at odds with

other miners. Their refusal in 1984 to take action without the sanc-
tion of a ballot was central in the defeat of the NUM. Not only did
they keep adding to coal stocks, but their creation of a breakaway
organisation, the Union of Democratic Miners, was at the heart of
what eventually amounted to the virtual destruction of the NUM.

What happened in 1926 perhaps exceeded in bitterness even
the rancid atmosphere that surrounded the resolution of the eighties dispute. Well, not even resolution, because in 1985, as in 1926,
in the aftermath of the General Strike, there was no deal, no agreement between the two sides. In both cases the outcome was in one
sense inconclusive. In the second instance you might even call it
suitably *Arthurian* in its ambiguity because there was no surrender, even if no one was in any doubt as to who had won and lost.

How much the past coloured the present had been amply
demonstrated when Lawrence Daly, the NUM General Secretary,
walked out of 10 Downing Street at one o clock in the morning of
February 19, 1972, and announced that the Britain's miners had
at last got their revenge for the events of 1926. It was an entirely
incredible event that reversed everyone's understanding of the
condition of the mining industry. Throughout the sixties the NUM
was written off by many observers as a spent force in a declining
industry. The idea that it actually had the power to outmanoeuvre
and then humiliate a government would have been dismissed a
crude fantasy. But Britain's miners had reinvented themselves as
the SAS of organised labour, something that was to have profound
political consequences.

On that occasion, once the government had found itself unable
to counter the impact of the flying pickets which were bringing the
country to a standstill, it had to find a traditional way out of the
dispute, although it didn't bring an entirely traditional response. It
appointed a judge, Lord Wilberforce, to head an inquiry into the
pay claim that had had every one of Britain's 280,000 miners on
strike since January 9. The well-tried system was simple enough:
faced with an impasse, governments would find a senior legal
figure, or perhaps a professor of industrial relations, to conduct an
entirely impartial inquiry, which, it was generally understood,
would award the workers concerned more or less what they
wanted. The government could say it hadn't conceded any general
principle while the workers, vindicated, would push off back to
work a day or two later.

In keeping with this convention, Lord Wilberforce delivered a verdict which for the most part accepted the miners' claim. As the details came through on that Friday afternoon, men on the picket lines seemed almost bowled over by the extent of their achievement, an unprecedented routing of the authorities. Yes, they said, they'd be back at work on Monday. But then something even more extraordinary happened.

The National Executive of the NUM met in London to consider the Wilberforce report. It seemed that it would simply be a matter of applying a rubber stamp. But they had by no means finished yet. Or at least a majority hadn't and by thirteen votes to twelve they rejected the report. They wanted more money. It was time to go to Downing Street.

One of the members of the National Executive was Dai Francis, a man whose direct and distinctive way of speaking, combined with the robust clarity of his views, made him probably the best-known trade union official in Wales. His son, Hywel, later told me about his father's account of what had happened that night.

The talks in Downing Street were held between the Prime Minister and his team on one side and the three national officials of the NUM on the other. They were in one room, the whole of the NUM National Executive were in another. Every time a concession was made, the negotiators went back and reported to the National Executive. The executive kept finding more concessions they wanted made.

"And they were quite major concessions," Hywel Francis recalled, "long-running grievances that my father's father had lost, going back to 1915 at least. They finally came back and said they'd run out of things to ask for."

At that point Dai, who'd taken a hard line throughout the talks, said that in that case he moved a return to work. But the Kent miners still weren't satisfied.

"No, no, no." they said. "We've got to wait."

"But we haven't got any more concessions to ask for."

"Yes, but just give us a bit more time and we can think of something."

In his autobiography, Joe Gormley confirms the mood if not those details. By midnight the negotiators had squeezed twenty new concessions from the government and the coal board. Even then they went back for one more, a detail of the wages system that had been a matter of dispute since nationalisation, twenty-five years previously. It would cost the NCB another eleven and a half million pounds but by now that was almost pocket money. It was conceded.

In those few triumphant hours in Westminster, I suppose, the pattern for the next thirteen years was set as an unprecedented mood of self-belief flooded through the leadership and the rank and file of the NUM. The reputation of the National Union of Mineworkers as the crack regiment of the class war was founded on those events. Two years later they were to consolidate that mystique in the most spectacular manner. Now, it seemed, they could do anything.

But not for long. By 1984 many of the factors that had given the miners a period of unprecedented power, a period that didn't last as long in reality as did the illusion built upon it, had been substantially eroded and were on the verge of being eliminated entirely. Coal mining in Britain had been in decline for a long time and was only following the path already travelled by other great industries – textiles, shipbuilding and steel among them. It lasted that much longer than some of them because it was propped up for strategic reasons that were rapidly disappearing and which were to be eliminated pretty well entirely by the end of the Cold War.

But mining retained its powerful grip on the public imagination. It was one of those occupations that filled onlookers with nervous admiration. Who in his senses would do such a job if he didn't have to? It was emblematic of a history stretching back two centuries and more, a history that was now in the process of being deleted from the national memory. This could be why Arthur Scargill, although often portrayed as a figure of fun, an eccentric howling at the socialist moon, is still sometimes represented as some kind of prophet, too. People look around and see that the coal mines have almost all disappeared, shrug their shoulders and say: "Arthur was right, you know".

In all this Mrs Thatcher filled the most valuable role a politician can perform: she was someone to blame. The battle between her government and the National Union of Mineworkers, commonly represented as a personal struggle between her and Arthur Scargill, stands for the overwhelming industrial and social upheaval that swept through Britain in the eighties and nineties. If Mrs Thatcher can be convicted of these crimes then everyone else, however much they knew these changes were inevitable, is clearly innocent. And there's nothing more revealing than the fact that her own party, struggling to rebuild its credibility in the twenty-first century, took care not to mention her name too often. It suited them as well to have a scapegoat for all the things they would have carried out and, in some cases, actually did carry out to redesign the shape of Britain. She has been airbrushed out of her own revolution as efficiently as if she had fallen foul of some Stalinist censor. At the end of 2005, Thatcherism, which had been looking pretty ragged for some years, joined public ownership and the unions in the box of discarded props. The man who put it there, David Cameron, had been nine years old when Margaret Thatcher became leader of the Conservative Party, six when Arthur Scargill stood at the Saltley gates.

But yet, you don't have to like Margaret Thatcher, or even admire her, to see what a difference she made through that year-long confrontation. Many of the consequences were, as we shall see, unintended. Certainly, for example, there's good reason to number her among the saviours of the Labour Party. And who would have guessed that the National Union of Mineworkers, perhaps the most male chauvinist organisation in the industrial world, and Margaret Thatcher, who by and large kept women out of her cabinet, would between them push dozens of women into the front line of public life?

In the end Mrs Thatcher led the country across a ravine and blew up the bridge behind her. In places like Wales, where the past is such a popular holiday resort, that has caused both terror and confusion but it has also compelled people to see how they might try to resolve the problems posed by their arrival in new territory. They cannot scramble back to the other side.

★

Towards the end of 2002, three of us took Philip Weekes to lunch in a restaurant overlooking Cardiff Bay. He was a bit deaf and using a stick but he remained a striking man, lean and silver-haired, still seeing to it that the manufacturers of Silk Cut cigarettes didn't go out of business, helping the rest of us make the same useful contribution to the welfare of the producers of Spanish wine.

Our only purpose in meeting was to gossip. We talked, for instance, about his adventures in flying. He would have much preferred to have been a pilot than a mining engineer. He'd joined the RAF during the war, learnt to fly, but then was sent back to the coalfield because his eyesight didn't meet the necessary standards. Thirty-nine years on he took it up again even though, as he said, he was probably twice the average age of the members of the flying club.

We also recalled some of the great incidents in the last decades of the South Wales coalfield, some of them dramatic, many more comic. Mostly our stories were about people. Did we remember the NCB director who, shortly after his retirement, was found to have had oil-fired central heating in his house? Then there was that consumptive-looking lodge secretary who was one of the few people in the entire industry Philip really hated. Why we had never got Philip on film saying to me for a news programme, as we'd long agreed, a coal board version of Lyndon Johnson's comment to a reporter: "What kind of chickenshit question is that to ask the President of the United States?" Then, was it true that one NUM official had a girlfriend whom he met regularly on the mountain between his home valley and hers? Why was there a persistent rumour that she had a wooden leg? Had we heard that, during one night of hilly passion, the official had lost his false teeth and the next day organised members of his office staff into a search party to look for them?

We talked on as the afternoon faded over the waters of what had once been one of the world's greatest ports. Ninety years before thirteen million tons of coal had been loaded onto ships here. In the same year a quarter of a million men in South Wales had mined fifty-seven million tons of the stuff. From then on the story had been one of slow but inexorable decline, a process tempered by the idea that surely this was one industry so massive that it could never disappear entirely. Now expensive toy boats for weekend sailors bobbed idly on a lagoon overlooked by a series of blocks of flats built specifically for the well-to-do.

I was aware then as it grew dark, perhaps we all were, that no newcomer would in future be able to join in our conversation about these familiar things. It really was all over.

WE'LL SUPPORT YOU EVERMORE

NOT MUCH MORE THAN six months elapsed between the end of the miners' strike in March 1985 and the speech Neil Kinnock made that was to revolutionise the Labour Party. Getting on for twenty years afterwards I asked Kinnock if had simply been a coincidence that the speech had followed so swiftly on that last, raw confrontation. His answer revealed how turning points in history often owe as much to chance as they do to the maps and charts of careful strategic analysis.

No one who was in the hall in Bournemouth on that day, Tuesday, October 1, 1985, is likely to forget it. In more than half a lifetime of listening to some of the most passionate and accomplished speakers in British public life I can't recall anything more compelling. Among other things it was a speech that reminded us that, far from being a substitute for action, as critics often assert, words can be just as powerful as deeds as instruments of change. In this case there are good reasons to believe that only Kinnock could have done it; certainly that he was the only person in the Labour Party at that time who could have achieved so much with a single speech. I don't say that because of his famous powers of oratory, which didn't always serve him well, particularly when he piled adjectives and adverbs and repetitions one on top of another as he built a teetering house of rhetorical cards. It was much more because of what he was, what he represented in the iconography of Labour folk history. Although we couldn't have known it at the time we were, in that hall on that day, witnessing the public beginning of a process that was to transform the British political landscape.

The ostensible object of Kinnock's attack on that occasion was a small, carefully-selected group of people, the supporters of the Trotskyite Militant Tendency who were a key influence in the conduct of the affairs of Liverpool City Council. At the same time, as almost everyone understood, this group also represented by extension any number of far left activists who were understandably accused of having brought the party to the brink of permanent electoral disaster. In Liverpool their specific transgression was refusing to make cuts in council services to conform to government spending limits. That refusal, on the grounds that such cuts would damage the lives of people in an area beset by social and economic difficulties, had brought the city to the edge of bankruptcy. Like Arthur Scargill, Militant believed that, faced with determined and ethically plausible opposition, Margaret Thatcher and her government would back away. Indeed they talked specifically of opening "a second front" that would eventually bring the government down.

In their pursuit of this objective, however, one of the consequences was, as financial disaster loomed, that they had to give notice to the council's 30,000 employees. It was this action that Kinnock made the focus of the onslaught in which he denounced the entire philosophy of the far left activists who had come to have such a powerful influence in the party. They had done so partly by establishing themselves in the smaller constituency organisations that were easily manipulated and intimidated, as well as in some of the local authorities like Liverpool, and in a number of the public service unions, notably in the white collar sector. What Kinnock specifically accused the Liverpool councillors of was dealing in what he described as "implausible promises".

Then he went on: "I'll tell you what happens with implausible promises. You start with far-fetched resolutions. They are then pickled into a rigid dogma, a code, and you go through the years sticking to that, outdated, misplaced, irrelevant to the real needs and you end in the grotesque chaos of a Labour council – a *Labour* council – hiring taxis to scuttle round a city handing out redundancy notices to its own workers."

There was a storm of applause. "I'm telling you..." Kinnock began again, but he was drowned out by the cheering and the whistling which was countered moments afterwards by booing from the Left whose members took a little while to grasp what was going on. Kinnock's words were carefully chosen, especially the deliberately insulting description of scuttling councillors which, he said later, had come from a childhood memory of black beetles, 'black pats', that emerged in the mornings from behind the cold ashes in the grate in his grandmother's house. You couldn't miss the element of disgust in his voice.

The cheering and the booing went on and on. Eric Heffer*, a Liverpool MP and a member of Labour's National Executive, strode from the platform in protest. Still the noise continued until, after almost a minute, Kinnock, brushing aside an unhelpful attempt at an intervention by the chairman, was able to resume.

"I'm telling you," he said, "no matter how entertaining, how fulfilling to short-term egos... I tell you and you'll listen... I'm telling you, you can't play politics with people's jobs, with people's services."

It had been more than six years since Labour had held office and it was to be another twelve before it did so again. But it's not an exaggeration to suggest that what Kinnock had to say on that October morning both prefigured the changes in the party that were to take place and revealed, in a few extraordinary minutes, how it was already changing, even as he spoke. The Left was taken aback by the force of the attack and the enthusiasm with which it was received by their critics and former victims. They suddenly realised that, for the first time in years they were now the object of the sectarian hatred that had long disfigured the party conferences. They had routinely jeered Labour ministers and MPs whom they accused of betraying socialism and selling out the working class. For the most part the objects of their scorn, huddled together in their designated seats, had looked on in meek silence. Only twelve months before the same conference had burst into an ecstasy of approval at Arthur Scargill's every word. Now the kind of people who thought Scargill was the Martin Luther of the trade union movement, preaching that salvation could be achieved by faith alone, were being told that, actually, they were the enemy. Kinnock might have been talking specifically about Militant, but his words applied more widely.

This was revealed in a debate the next day that was in its way equal in importance to the anti-Militant speech. The conference considered a proposal that a future Labour government should reimburse the fines imposed on the NUM during the year-long strike and that miners who had been sacked for misconduct should be reinstated. Kinnock was completely opposed to the idea but the National Executive was sympathetic. When they discussed the resolution before it went to the conference the NEC was more

---

* Roy Hattersley records that Michael Foot once said of Heffer: "I used to think of him as a noble savage but I was only half right."

or less evenly split. Kinnock's biographer, Martin Westlake, records that Kinnock leant across to Michael Meacher, a left-wing MP, later to be a minister under Tony Blair.

"Michael," Kinnock said, "if this vote goes the wrong way you can say goodbye to any prospect of a Labour government". With Meacher's mind thus concentrated, his vote followed and the motion was defeated by fifteen votes to fourteen. In the conference itself the resolution was eventually passed, but by fewer than three to two. That meant that it didn't have a big enough majority to be included automatically in the party's next manifesto. That sort of thing mattered deeply in those days, in sharp contrast to the tooth-less condition of the contemporary Labour conference. The mood of division was illustrated most vividly by Eric Hammond, the leader of the electricians' union, who described the miners as "lions led by donkeys". Such a remark could hardly have made Hammond, a right-winger, any more unpopular with most of the rest of the trade union movement than he already was. But that he could say such a thing at all revealed how fragile was the solidarity that figured so largely in union mythology; an illusion of course, but for a long time it had been a comforting one. Eric Hammond would soon take a central role in demonstrating just how ephemeral it was.

★

The importance of those two conference days didn't simply lie in the bold efforts to start pushing back (or pushing out) the far left, but also in the way in which Kinnock and his supporters spelt out a vital aspect of a parliamentary democracy that Militant, like Arthur Scargill, had tried to subvert. They had argued, in effect, that there were some actions governments weren't allowed to take, whatever their constitutional legitimacy. Closing pits was one of them, cutting services in Liverpool another. This was a period when, frustrated by their inability to compel the government to alter its course through traditional political methods, activists called for the increased use of what was known as extra-parlia-mentary activity. So in Liverpool they wouldn't set budgets that met government rules. In a different way the miners argued that, if defeated and punished by a Conservative government, they could nevertheless have their losses restored some time in the future by a Labour administration.

Such arguments had been heard before. In the seventies, for example, when some local authorities, most famously Clay Cross in Derbyshire, were penalised for refusing to implement the Conservatives' Fair Rents Act for council housing. Kinnock recognised how dangerous a path this might be because it undermined the central principle of the British system of government. If Conservative measures were to be disobeyed as lacking legitimacy, with legitimacy to be decided by the Militant Tendency or the National Union of Mineworkers, you would be sure that any future Labour government would be repaid in the same coin. In the debate on compensating the miners for their losses Kinnock argued that it would be dishonest for the party to say "that somehow people can come into conflict with the common law, the civil law, the criminal law. And one day, some time in the future, the cavalry will ride in in the form of a Labour government and pick up the tab."

In fact it's not strictly accurate to say that these events marked the very beginning of a radically new mood in the Labour Party although this was certainly the time when that began to become clear. Their origins perhaps lay a year or so earlier, but the timing of these events, which was out of Kinnock's hands, was to give them a particular momentum. And equally important was the fact that they came from a leader who was able to deploy a powerful personal authority in this regard, raising the question, as I have said, whether anyone but Kinnock could have done it.

Kinnock represented, almost to the point of caricature, the kind of person of which many Labour people liked to believe their party was largely composed. He was the son of a miner, recognisably, even ostentatiously, Welsh. He was (or had been) an old-fashioned left winger, pursuing at full volume the tradition by which such people reserved their most vehement criticisms for their own party. He had been a particularly effective opponent of policies close to the heart of the party establishment, including devolution and membership of the Common Market. In such ways he could be seen as an heir of the most famous Welsh rebel of them all, Aneurin Bevan. Like Bevan he was a brilliant orator and, also like Bevan, he came from Tredegar. He had never held office and so, in the eyes of the many internal critics of the Labour governments of the seventies, he had clean hands. He was, for example, free of any blame for one of the left's most hated events, the 1976 cuts in public spending on the say-so of the International

Monetary Fund. He was just a step out of the working class and
not, like most Labour leaders, a public schoolboy or Oxford don
or lawyer. He was attractive, gregarious and funny. He might have
been to university but, as some elements in the political world are
still inclined to say, *only to Cardiff*. To this day it remains the case
that no British Prime Minister who has been to university has been
to a university other than Oxford or Cambridge.

In short the message was this: if such a man was engaged in a
struggle with people who proclaimed themselves the true heirs of
socialism, the keepers of the holy flame, then there was a serious
battle in progress in which it was impossible not to take sides.
Kinnock's background also helped his cause in a less obvious way.
It combined with his inexperience as leader to create an unpredictable (and at the time unwelcome) set of circumstances that
opened the way to the beginning of a great upheaval. What it did,
in not much more than a decade, was to render the Labour Party
pretty well entirely unrecognisable to those who'd followed its
rackety journey through the twentieth century. Perhaps the least
likely event to take place in British politics, then or now, would be
for Neil Kinnock to thank Arthur Scargill for his help, but such an
acknowledgement would nevertheless not be entirely out of place.

This arises because Kinnock's original plan had been to launch
his attack on Militant the previous year – at the party conference
in October 1984. It would, he said, have been the ideal time to
have taken them on. But by that time the miners' strike had been
in progress for more than six months.

"The sentiment of the Labour Party, for reasons I understood," he said, "was such that any attempt to take on Militant at
that stage would just have turned into farce. So I had to bide my
time. The first opportunity that arose, because the only place to
take this action was obviously in front of the whole Labour Party,
brought together, was in October 1985. I must say it stretched my
patience but it would have been a real charge of the Light Brigade
to have tried it in October 1984. The Labour Party would have
been devastated by a failure in 1984."

But the miners' strike didn't simply provide a temporary
obstacle to Kinnock's plans for reform. It also presented him with
a personal dilemma in which, for once, indecisiveness turned out
to be the most strategically sound form of behaviour. What looked
like a disastrous intervention by the NUM proved to be a golden

opportunity. Kinnock had been Labour leader for only six months or so when the strike began and he was beginning a process of rebuilding the party as a credible political force. It was deeply divided, electorally unpopular, even, people seriously thought, mortally wounded.

For a long time a favoured analysis in some sections of the Labour Party was that Conservative election victories, even Conservative majorities of 144, contained a single incontrovertible lesson. That was that people voted Tory only because Labour policies weren't left-wing enough. Victory in the class war, it was argued, could only be won by aims that directly contradicted the capitalist philosophy of the other side. They had certainly put that theory to the test in 1983 with a manifesto that contained the long-cherished dreams of the left. Its main proposals included leaving the Common Market, unilateral nuclear disarmament, abolishing the House of Lords and substantially extending public ownership. It was most famously described by the Labour MP and former minister, Gerald Kaufman, as the longest (thirty-three pages) suicide note in history. The result was that the Social Democrats, created by senior Labour Party defectors, in alliance with the Liberals, came within a couple of per cent of pushing Labour into third place in the general election.

It's easy to see why, less than a year after this fiasco, any miners' strike would have been, to say the least, unhelpful. For some demoralised members of the Labour Party it might have been a slightly cheering reminder of glorious victories of a decade or so previously, but for the average voter it would probably only re-awaken memories of the grim days of the winter of discontent. That would have been bad enough but this strike might have been carefully choreographed to cause the party maximum damage even among those voters who admired the miners and who thought they should be well paid for doing a tough and unattractive job. Paradoxically they might have been more sympathetic to a dispute over money rather than one over principle.

In these circumstances, then, what was Neil Kinnock to do? Here he was, son of a miner and all the rest of it, a man whose origins and career insisted that he should provide the political inspiration for the NUM's industrial muscle. He says now that he didn't make the right decision but he might argue that he didn't make the wrong one either. He kept his distance and let matters take their fateful course. He shared a platform with Scargill on a number of occasions but he stayed away from the picket lines and he resisted repeated efforts to tie him, and hence the Labour Party, into the miners' campaign. On November 1, for example, the NUM invited him and Norman Willis, the TUC General Secretary, to attend five rallies. The next day Labour's National Executive endorsed the idea that Kinnock should be at those rallies. A day later his office announced that, because of 'pressure of work', he was unlikely to attend.

Reflecting on those events now, though, he now considers that he made one central mistake: that was in not calling on the NUM to hold a ballot at the beginning of the strike. Twenty years on he regretted his failure to act.

"I should have called for a ballot at the very beginning. The moment I heard that the miners' conference, under the advice of Scargill, had changed its constitution – quite properly in my view – to make it possible to have a national strike on the basis of a majority of 50 per cent and then secondly decided not to have a ballot – the moment I heard that I should have said: 'Without a ballot this strike is doomed. It is critical for the future of coal that a ballot is held.'"

Of course the important question that then arises is this: if Kinnock had demanded a ballot would the NUM National Executive have paid any attention? There's no doubt that continuing the union's long-established reputation as an organisation that respected the authority of a majority vote would have enhanced its case in the eyes of the public. But Scargill clearly could not risk holding a ballot he might well lose and consequently the utter destruction of his plans. As Kinnock says, what was going on was something outside the traditional nature of British industrial disputes, however bitterly some of them might have been contested.

"It was the inescapable fact that they were two contestants [Arthur Scargill and Margaret Thatcher] at the leadership of two strands in British society, effectively two sets of forces that were determined to make it a fight to the death. My criticism of Scargill was that he led his troops into the jaws of certain defeat simply because he did not employ the one weapon that really could have given him both moral standing and his argument moral standing and political effectiveness."

Instead the moral standing was seized by those miners who

went on working. However much Scargill waved the NUM rule book in support of his contention that the strike was perfectly legitimate, it was clear to the public, who, after all, had had the miners' mythology rammed down their throats at every possible opportunity, that people should not be compelled to strike without being allowed to vote on the matter. Yes, it happened in other unions, but not in the NUM.

In its turn that failure of democracy led to perhaps the unhappiest aspect of the entire dispute, the violence that broke out as one group of miners turned on another. It's possible to see now that, among all the other great shifts that were taking place in industrial life, the scenes that played out on the television night after night were to have a significant effect on the entire trade union movement.

"Violence on the picket line certainly changed me," Kim Howells recalled later. "I helped to organise pickets all over the country and being there among that violence and seeing one group of workers throwing bricks and abuse and vitriol against another group of workers just went against everything I'd been brought up to believe in. There was no sense of dialogue. There was a sense of loathing and hatred. Where it impacted most on me was in instances where men had been on strike perhaps for nine months and couldn't stand any more. They'd been under enormous pressure from their families and had gone back to work. They had been very, very brave men who finally, for whatever reason, couldn't do it any more and they'd gone into work. For them to be vilified in the way they were I thought was the product of a bankrupt strategy."

Sometimes the battles between those who struck and those who worked touched on the edge of comedy. One of the two remaining pits in north Wales went on strike; at the other the men continued to work. When his wife and young son were threatened, Ted McKay, the union's regional secretary, a member of the NUM National Executive and an opponent of the strike, was forced to go into hiding. He decided the best place to hide was in south Wales since he felt his pursuers wouldn't look for him in Britain's most solidly strike-bound coalfield.

But there weren't many jokes. When, at a rally in Aberavon, the TUC's amiable leader Norman Willis spoke out against violence on the picket lines, a hangman's noose was lowered from the gallery above his head. Two weeks after that a taxi driver, David

Wilkie, was killed as he drove a working miner to a pit near Merthyr Tydfil. Two strikers had thrown a concrete block on to his cab from a bridge across the road.

Arguments persist to this day over who was responsible for the violence. Was it provoked by over-eager policing? Did it suit the government to have it continue as part of a deliberate strategy to discredit the NUM? Were there, as some senior strike supporters claim, soldiers dressed as police involved? Was coverage of these events deliberately distorted by the broadcasters to make it look as though miners had attacked police on occasions when the reverse was true? It's difficult to say even if you were there, impossible if you were not.

What we do know is that in these circumstances people are certainly capable of acting in ways that can shock you. Years before, during the 1972 strike, I'd gone early one morning to report on events in Tondu, near Bridgend, at the west Wales headquarters of the coal board. Miners were picketing clerks who were continuing to go into work. For half an hour press and pickets were involved in genial conversation as we waited for what seemed likely to be a token protest. But then, as cars approached the gates, the mood darkened. The clerical workers, practically all of them women, cowered and wept as men banged on the roofs of their vehicles, pushing and shoving, violent and abusive. It was nothing by the standards of the confrontations we were to become used to, but in its way it was fearsome. Not an ounce of coal would be dug or moved because these women went to work; they weren't even members of the NUM's clerical section, but still they provoked a towering and uncharacteristic rage.

There's no denying that the emergence of such fury not only affected attitudes towards the 1984-85 strike itself, but it might well have been one of the factors that contributed to fresh attitudes to the unions as a whole from a shoulder-shrugging acceptance and occasional exasperation to a sense of suspicion and resentment. And such a new mood could be found within some of the unions as well as outside them, not surprisingly among those asked by Arthur Scargill to sacrifice their own jobs to defend those of the miners. In December 1984, after nine months of the strike, one opinion poll showed that 21 per cent of those questioned sympathised with the miners while 51 per cent said they agreed with the coal board.

What also seemed to have ebbed away during the previous

decade was some of the regard in which the wider British public had always held the miners. It came in part from the respect paid to the nature of their work as well as the influence of the mining diaspora, the links with the industry taken to the rest of Britain by ex-colliers who had been forced to look elsewhere for work during the lean days of the twenties and thirties. Now it seems as though the miners were in thrall to their own heroic legend as spelt out by Scargill, comforting themselves with a belief in their powerful grip on the affections of the wider British public. Hywel Francis believes that this was perhaps their leader's greatest mistake. "What Arthur Scargill didn't understand was that it's been estimated that only about 30 per cent of the British public supported the miners, although it appeared to be very different if you were standing with a collecting tin in Porth or in Neath. But the reality was that out there in southern England and in the parts of the country which we needed to win in general elections they were quite hostile to the miners."

At that stage, too, we were well advanced on the de-industrialisation of Britain. Many people, especially the young, were increasingly unfamiliar with the nature of manual work. Among those taking notice was Kim Howells. "I remember very clearly in the strike going up to London with some other boys.* And we drove through the City on a beautiful day, beautiful blue skies. We were agape. It must have been about four o clock in the afternoon and outside these huge buildings were all these young men and women dressed in these clothes like we'd never seen before, drinking champagne. And we just couldn't believe there was an economic boom going on in 84-85. Parts of the country were experiencing economic growth which they hadn't seen for a lifetime. We didn't believe there were other parts of the country like that. But there were and they were voting for Thatcher."

*

We have to remember that the official version of the relationship between the unions and the rest of the Labour movement was a useful fiction, a romance, as much as it was a reflection of real life.

---

* In South Wales-speak 'boys' doesn't mean young people under the age of sixteen but any male person who is the same age or younger than the speaker, however old he might happen to be.

This was no lifelong love affair but a tempestuous marriage in which the most familiar sound was that of flying crockery. Divorce was unthinkable, living together frequently impossible. It was no wonder that the Welsh politician, Ray Gunter, said gloomily, when Harold Wilson appointed him Minister of Labour, that the job was "a bed of nails". It was curious, too, that the one serious effort by Labour to undo this state of affairs should have come from the left of the party; odder still that the move was eventually scuppered from the right.

In her 1969 white paper, *In Place of Strife*, Barbara Castle, Secretary of State for Employment and Productivity and the long-time heroine of the Labour left, proposed the introduction of penal sanctions in an attempt to curb unofficial strikes. She had some unexpected supporters, not least Tony Benn, then Minister of Technology and an eager moderniser. On January 1, 1969, she recorded in her diary: "I rang Wedgie about my proposals. He replied cheerfully, 'I'm your friend.'" And in the difficulties that followed, acrimonious even by Labour Party standards, Benn was a loyal ally.

The most effective opposition, which was eventually to destroy Mrs Castle's plans, came from Jim Callaghan, then Home Secretary, who put on an astonishing display of disregard for the conventions of government, in particular the idea that members of the Cabinet should embrace collective responsibility once a policy decision had been taken.

At a meeting of Labour's National Executive committee he simply ignored this protocol and voted against government policy to introduce legislation based on *In Place of Strife*. The Prime Minister, Harold Wilson, said, yes, he was going to take action over this flagrant breach of the rules. Callaghan would be punished in some unspecified way, but not just yet. In the end, a few months later, Wilson expelled him from the inner cabinet, a move that had more in the way of public symbolism than practical effect. Callaghan considered resigning but didn't do so. Soon enough many more colleagues were abandoning Barbara Castle and her white paper.

Somewhere in heaven today Callaghan, a one-time union official is no doubt getting his reward, his every need assiduously attended to by members of the National Association of Cherubim and Seraphim, but he certainly didn't get it on earth. Having wrecked a Conservative administration the unions went on, even-handedly, to make a substantial contribution to arranging the same fate for the Labour government of which he was leader.

Callaghan's opposition to *In Place of Strife* came from a typically shrewd combination of principle, rational assessment and
political calculation. There was, for example, the consideration
that he was at that time treasurer of the Labour Party and, as a
general election approached, it would have been more than a little
insensitive to offend the very people who were supposed to find
large sums of money for the campaign. He also recognised that not
only would penal sanctions do little or nothing to curb unofficial
strikes but in fact they would almost certainly make matters worse.
Not only would strikers and unions face the prospect of being
taken to court but the government itself would have to make the
order taking them there. That the consequence would inevitably be
direct confrontation between the unions and the government was
to be demonstrated only a few years later when striking London
dockers piled into the Heath government's version of industrial
relations legislation and reduced what was left of it to rubble.

But although Callaghan might have been correct in his analysis
of the proposals, their failure nevertheless left unanswered perhaps
the biggest question all British governments faced in domestic
policy: how could they find a method of persuading the unions to
co-operate in the running of a workable economic strategy. It was
a long time before the answer was revealed. Since it couldn't be
done with the unions it would have to be done without them.

Over the decades since the war successive governments had
invented any number of seductive titles for what was essentially
the same policy: pay restraint. From Selwyn Lloyd's Pay Pause in
1961 and his Guiding Light in 1962 to Labour's Social Contract
in 1974 they were all after the same thing, sometimes by attempts
to reach agreement, at other times through the law. Under the
Wilson government of 1966-70, there was a "period of severe
restraint" followed by a "period of moderation" which in turn was
followed by a wage freeze or, you might have said, a period of total
restraint. In 1972 the Heath government introduced a pay policy
(Counter Inflation [Temporary Provisions] Bill) when it had
sworn never to do anything of the kind. Where Wilson had a Prices
and Incomes Board, Heath had a Pay Award and Price
Commission. The consequence for Heath in the end, as we know,
was the policy-busting miners' strike and his reluctant departure
from Downing Street.

These policies were never effective other than for a very short time, not least because they involved governments directly in matters they were not equipped to resolve, attempting to police pay settlements in every industry, private and public, throughout the country. It was a circus and it's simply extraordinary to read now about the forlorn attempts to micro-manage the business of putting a lid on pay claims. In his diary entry for November 17, 1968, Richard Crossman, then the Social Services Secretary, wrote about Barbara Castle, the Secretary of State for Employment and Productivity, and her doomed efforts to keep the show on the road. "She is working hard but despite this she is wearing herself out in a frantic effort to plug the holes in the dam and prevent the wage increases rushing through in an overwhelming torrent. By the end of the week she had just managed to get the building trades operatives to refer their claim to the Prices and Incomes Board but she still has the bank clerks wanting seven and a half per cent. She is going to give them three and a half per cent and looming ahead is a crisis with ICI. These awards can't be held back and as a result the whole prices and incomes policy will collapse. The terrible thing here is really that it has collapsed. Public opinion and the unions have won."

Crossman adds a little later: "People know we are licked and Barbara just struggles, struggles to hold on and try to operate a policy which is detested, which has riven us from our own supporters, separated us from the unions and is creating the biggest split inside the PLP and inside the Labour Party. "So much of the Government's energy is concentrated on keeping this completely unreal, unworkable policy going. We relaxed our grip after devaluation and, having done so, we then tried to reimpose it in the stringent post-devaluation conditions. The one thing you can't do is reimpose a prices and incomes policy once you have relaxed it. It's only fair to say that Roy (Jenkins, Chancellor of the Exchequer) never believed in the policy but he realized that he couldn't at that moment take the lid off the pressure cooker because the mere removal of the lid is itself dangerous."

Perhaps governments are by nature slow learners or maybe they keep on doing the same things over and over again because they have only a very small number of ideas at their disposal. Ten years after Crossman wrote those words, the lid blew off the government's pay policy and the bubbling casserole ended up splattered around the kitchen walls in an event, or series of events, that made up the winter of discontent. It was something that finally exploded the idea that the objectives of trade unions and governments could coincide for anything other than strictly limited periods of time.

There's a general if not universal assumption that, no matter what decisions he had taken, Callaghan would have lost the 1979 general election. But just in case there was any doubt the unions turned it into a certainty; not on purpose, perhaps, but because they couldn't help themselves doing what unions had always done, just as the government did what governments had always done. A curious incident in the approach to that famous winter showed how severely relations had been damaged.

There is considerable ambiguity in subsequent explanations of what happened on that afternoon in Brighton but no one who was there can have failed to see the failure of the political and industrial sides of the Labour Party to engage with each other, even to speak the same language. On September 5, Jim Callaghan rose on the platform to speak to the TUC's annual congress.

Virtually everyone present was expecting a general election that autumn. The government had no majority; the Lib-Lab pact that had helped sustain it in office had been formally concluded; the opinion polls were reasonably encouraging and there was no immediate crisis in sight. Callaghan was due to make a television broadcast on September 7 in which, commentators felt certain, he would make the necessary announcement. Already that week the unions had been preparing for an October election, digging into their funds to provide the money for Labour to fight it. Surely in these circumstances there'd be at least a hint, perhaps more, of his intentions.

What actually took place was remarkable even by the colourful standards long established in the state of alternative reality in which many political conferences take place. The audience sat unsympathetically through Callaghan's case for a five per cent ceiling on pay rises. Then, unexpectedly and astonishingly, he sang to them. More accurately, he spoke-sang, like Rex Harrison in *My Fair Lady*, giving them part of an old music hall song which began, "There was I waiting at the church... " and ended, "Can't get away to marry you today. My wife won't let me." And then he laughed and his audience applauded in a hesitant manner that revealed their incomprehension. What on earth could this mean? Who was going to be waiting at the church? Was it the TUC? Or the Labour Party?

Or Mrs Thatcher? The whole thing was so baffling that most people simply assumed that the laugh was on someone else and that the election would take place as anticipated.

Two days later I sat in a television studio with a group of politicians including Jack Brooks (later Lord Brooks of Tremorfa), who was Callaghan's agent in Cardiff South East. We were waiting to discuss the prospects for the forthcoming election which would, we all confidently assumed, be announced in the Prime Ministerial broadcast that immediately preceded our programme. Oh well, there were we, waiting at the church...

And here we come to another of those tantalising what if? questions of the period. What if, instead of simply teasing and annoying the unions with his little joke, Callaghan had gone on to call a general election? And then won it? Unlikely, has to be the verdict on that. In any case, another virtually invisible majority or another hung parliament, probably the best he could hope for, would almost certainly have been too much for Callaghan himself and the Parliamentary Labour Party. Fatigue would have got them pretty soon. But suppose he'd called the election and Mrs Thatcher had won by a decent margin. Might Labour history have been rewritten, might the Labour movement have been diverted from the disastrous course on which it was embarked? In those circumstances the most damaging confrontation in history between a Labour government and the unions would have been averted.

And so the hypothetical questions multiply. Without the winter of discontent and the impetus it gave to the battle between the left and right in the Labour Party, isn't it more likely that Callaghan would have been succeeded, not by Michael Foot, but by Denis Healey? As Roy Hattersley wrote later: "Had Denis Healey been elected Labour leader, the political history of Britain would have been different. He might not have carried the party to victory in 1983. But we would have been beaten, not annihilated, and during the following five years he would have led a convincing recovery."

You might argue, though, that what Labour actually needed at that time was what it got: the disastrous period of Michael Foot's leadership between 1980 and 1983, a period of such anguish for Labour moderates that some left the party to form the SDP while others were left to face up to the measures necessary to return Labour to the political mainstream. It all got so bad that people could no longer pretend it could all be mended with sticking plaster and a few stitches. In those circumstances it seems unlikely, too, that Neil Kinnock, Michael Foot's friend and protégé, would have succeeded Healey as party leader. Thus Kinnock would not have been in a position to make the crucial contribution he did, on October 1,1985, and subsequently, to the reshaping of the party. And again, without the intervention of the miners' strike his freedom to manoeuvre would have been more restricted.

"People have argued that without the defeat that that strike brought there probably wouldn't have been a Tony Blair and a Labour victory," Kim Howells says. "Because, of course, to put it at its most brutal, the trade union movement needed to learn that the victories of the seventies were a thing of the past."

Then he adds: "I'm not sure I believe that, but it is argued."

During the strike Kim was among the loudest voices in the NUM condemning Kinnock for his failure to offer the union unequivocal backing. Later he went in for a period of revision. "I became incredibly frustrated with him during the course of the strike and said some horrible things about him." Indeed he did, and one of the things he said was this: "There are many people inside the NUM who find it extraordinary when they regard Neil Kinnock's statements during this strike that he doesn't employ his undoubted powers for once to put the case clearly and to put it simply and to state his unequivocal support for the miners rather than attempt to emulate, in the way that he seems bent on doing, the windbags who occupy the majority of seats in parliament these days."

Twenty years later Kim took a rather more statesmanlike view of the man who had become a parliamentary colleague. Kinnock was, he said, in a difficult position. "He was fighting Militant and all kinds of nutters on the one side literally for the life and death of the Labour Party. Looking back on it one can argue endlessly about the role of Neil Kinnock. I think that in general he took precisely the right action. I've no doubt that the catastrophic defeat of the miners in 1985 made Neil determined to take on these adventurers – this is what they were, people like Scargill and the Militant Tendency – and say, 'Look, this is where it gets you'."

★

The campaign against Militant began in the context of a determination by the Labour leadership to assert itself against the anarchic left and at the same time find a way to a new relationship with the unions. The miners had, entirely inadvertently, opened the door to the pursuit of that strategy. Their defeat was a catharsis for the party and for other unions, as important for its symbolism as much as for its practical consequences, that sent a chill of foreboding through the whole movement. When the strike ended Mark Serwotka was a twenty-year-old living in Aberdare. Over the next couple of decades he made progress through the public sector organisation, the Civil and Public Services Union, which represents large numbers of clerical workers in the civil service. He is certainly no New Labour man and he became the union's General Secretary on an Independent Socialist ticket only after an acrimonious battle in the courts with the man he defeated. He sees the time of miners' strike as one of the most influential periods in the whole course of trade union history. "I think in the leadership of many of the trade unions the conclusion was reached that you can't actually win. I think that moulded the stances many of the trade unions actually took. What actually took hold was, well, if the miners can't beat a Conservative government then nobody can. It marked a period when nobody had the confidence to go forward with what in many cases were reasonable demands because they thought they were unlikely to be successful."

Another spectacular defeat for the unions was to follow and, in its way, it was perhaps as vital an event for the whole movement as was that of the miners. To some extent, Hywel Francis argues, one was the logical consequence of the other. "The most supportive of the miners of all the organised working class were the print unions because they knew that if the miners were defeated the government was going to be coming for them afterwards, which is exactly what happened with the demise of Fleet Street and the coming of Wapping within a year or so. So they knew that the praetorian guard, as people called the miners, once they were removed there was going to be inevitably a moving in against other well-organised industrial workers."

The stranglehold that members of the print unions exerted over the production of newspapers was a scandal. I was going to write that it was a public scandal but, outside the industry, few people knew how deeply corrupt it was because, naturally, you never read about it in the newspapers. Printing was an occupation, notoriously in Fleet Street but in other parts of the country too, in which non-existent people drew large extra pay packets under the names, among others, of Donald Duck and Mickey Mouse. Additional payments were also extorted by the engineering of production breakdowns which could only be repaired by the application of ready cash. Jobs that had long been replaced by expensive machines were still filled by men who stood silently and idly by. Those who nominally worked four shifts a week probably turned up only for two. And so on.

It was a coincidence, but also a sign of the times, that it was in February 1985, just as the miners strike was coming to an end, that Rupert Murdoch told his senior executives that he planned to establish a new plant at Wapping where he would be publishing a new newspaper called the *London Post*. It was a fiction, the cover for an astounding coup that in 1986 saw him move production of all his British titles, including the *Sun* and the *Times*, to the new operation. Crucially, in the operation to take apart one lot of unions he got the eager co-operation of another, the electricians of the EETPU.

Another of those sacred texts of organised labour was that one union shouldn't poach jobs from another. Eric Hammond, the General Secretary of the EETPU, and the man who had described the miners as being led by donkeys, made a spectacular wreck of that idea. He agreed privately with Murdoch that his members would run the new Wapping plant. The printers in Fleet Street, believing that they were too powerful to be defied by a mere proprietor, had no idea that a few miles away the future of newspapers was being reconstructed. Five hundred electricians (taking the place, incidentally, of six thousand printers) were to demonstrate that mass-circulation newspapers could be produced perfectly well by inexperienced people trained swiftly and secretly in modern methods of printing. The craft mysteries of ink and hot metal crumbled away, like Dracula exposed to the light of the rising sun.

As for solidarity: journalists envied and resented printers because of their formidable power, their rigid industrial disciplines (a journalist even laying a finger on a piece of type could bring the whole place to an immediate standstill) and their large pay packets swollen by those various traditional dodges and fiddles. When the time came they also recalled that printers had in the past always been perfectly happy to cross journalists' picket lines without a backward glance. It was for such reasons that Rupert Murdoch's editorial staffs voted to go to Wapping. Some refused, but many helped drive the nails into the coffins of the members of the National Graphical Association, the Society of Graphical and Allied Trades and the rest of them. Much as Arthur Scargill had taken a dynastic view of the coal industry, printers tended to believe that the chief function of newspapers was to provide jobs for printers. For more than a year they picketed and demonstrated outside the News International plant – Fortress Wapping as it became known – in a last struggle to maintain this remarkable principle. Their protest was broken by members of other unions making their way through the wreckage of Arthur Scargill's first commandment: "Thou shalt not cross a picket line". In the end they had to settle but, their skills suddenly a redundant part of industrial history, they were never to work in the newspaper trade again. In Rupert Murdoch the print unions had met someone smarter than they were and even tougher. So had the electricians. Despite their central role in making Wapping possible they were never granted negotiating rights with News International.

There was one odd footnote to this affair. In a curiously anachronistic gesture Neil Kinnock, who had been fiercely criticised by some people for his failure to put his personal authority squarely behind the miners' cause, did offer some support to the print unions. He instructed Labour MPs not to speak to journalists from the Murdoch papers. Most of them took no notice; being politicians they could no more resist talking to a reporter, any reporter, than they could turn down a free drink, so they'd probably have ignored the ban anyway. Nevertheless it was a strange thing for Kinnock to do when you consider than the unaccountable printers were probably a greater threat to democracy than the unballoted miners. If the compositors of the national press didn't think something should be published then it usually wasn't. For example, in his autobiography the former *Sunday Times* editor, Andrew Neil, records an incident during the Wapping dispute. The *Observer* intended to run a book review written by Bernard Levin, then a *Times* columnist. The editor, Donald Trelford, was told by the printers, as Neil puts it, "no Levin review or there will be no *Observer*". The management, as managements had done down the century, surrendered to the unions.

No one is going to start putting up statues of Rupert Murdoch in honour of his contribution to the cause of free speech but at least he gave previously supine owners a chance to demonstrate a little more enthusiasm for the principle. Murdoch himself was typically adaptable. He was the man who, because it threatened his Chinese business interests, decided his organisation wouldn't publish the autobiography of the Hong Kong governor, Chris Patten. Nor was he (at that time anyway) a friend of the Labour Party, but attitudes to newspaper proprietors were among the many things that were to be transformed by the tumultuous events of this period.

What happened to the print unions was a startling example to their colleagues in other industries. All unions found their ability to exert industrial power undermined by a series of events, only some of which were specifically aimed at reducing their influence. The six Acts of Parliament dealing with labour relations passed between 1980 and 1993 were clearly very influential, enforcing secret ballots, ending the closed shop and, perhaps most important of all, removing the unions' legal immunity and making their funds liable to sequestration if they broke the rules. But those new laws were underpinned by an economic revolution. State industries were privatised and so the government effectively removed itself from all those arguments about pay and conditions. The tea things had been cleared away at No.10 and the TUC and its members were told to find their own beer and sandwiches.

And then, as the twentieth century drew to a close, the collapse of the Soviet Union and the opening up of the old iron curtain countries, combined with the information technology revolution that fuelled the increasing globalisation of industry, transformed the nature of employment in Britain. If they wanted to remain competitive, manufacturers had no choice but to establish manu-facturing bases in places like the Czech Republic and Malaysia. Retailers had to look for the cheapest sources of supply, almost always abroad. Service industries built their call centres in coun-tries like India where well-educated and relatively low-paid staff were available in large numbers. The new world order meant, too, that governments no longer felt it necessary to maintain major British industries, like coal and steel, for strategic reasons.

The last remnant of the British-owned motor industry, for decades in its slow and painful decline a byword for trade union anarchy and management incompetence, went into receivership at the end of this period, in April 2004. You could tell how different the world had become when you reflected that Rover was going down the plughole at a vital stage of a general election campaign

and no one was seriously suggesting that the answer was for the
state to hand over bags of cash and keep the whole thing going in
the public sector. Yet thirty years previously that would have been
the routine response of a Labour government; probably, indeed, of
a Conservative one.

We can see how our entire political system has been remodelled
in a manner that might go a long way towards explaining the inability of many people at the beginning of the twenty-first century to
recognise the connection between the way in which they vote and
the manner in which they're governed. And this is true as much as
anything because of the role of the Labour Party. It would be
extravagant to argue that the new attitude stemmed solely from the
miners' strike, but that conflict was very influential; it provided one
of those road junctions where the driver had to make a crucial decision about the course the journey should now take.

The result has been that, contrary to all past experience, a
Labour government has made no effort of any kind, not even a
modest gesture, to restore any of the ground that was lost by the
unions under four successive Conservative governments. Not a
single clause has been repealed from the labour relations legislation, not one privatised industry (except the railways, up to a
grudging and unexpected point) has been taken back into public
ownership. People we once called bloated plutocrats are now, in
modern terminology, described as fat cats. They remain despised
of course, but still much safer than their predecessors from the
penal tax regimes that were once so popular with Labour progres-
sives. No one is seriously working out how to take their money
away from them. The Labour Party itself has moved to curb the
arbitrary authority of union leaders in its own affairs by introducing a system of one member one vote.

Tony Blair might have a reputation for insincerity but even he
had never been known to express the traditional sentimental
attachment to the unions as stout defenders of the British worker.
In that abstinence, indeed, he was very like Lady Thatcher. Instead
he was the man who got Clause IV removed from the party's
constitution. Everyone could recite it – a Labour government
would secure for the workers by hand or by brain the fruits of their
industry and the most equitable distribution thereof as may be
possible upon the basis of the common ownership of the means of
production, distribution and exchange.

Like many a familiar liturgy, the words had long since ceased
to have any meaning for most of those who uttered them, something that perhaps only increased the fervour with which they
were pronounced. It's revealing, I think, that commentators so
often compare it and its resonant phrases with a Biblical text. The
practical effect of its erasure was nil, but its symbolic importance
was in the way it snapped a thread connecting the present with the
past. It was the moment when Labour stopped even pretending
that such a thing was going to happen.

It's difficult to think of any other single item of policy that went
so clearly to the emotional heart of what Labour believers had
cherished for so long. That was why Tony Blair, in his first conference speech as leader in October 1994, used this issue as an
instrument to challenge the traditionalists. It was, as the spin
doctor jargon has it, a defining moment, a rebranding, a clear
statement of what kind of politician he was and what kind of party
he intended to lead. He did it early, he did it fast and consequently,
as people argued at the time, he did it without looking too deeply
at its implications. But if he'd thought more about it, if he'd spent
more time discussing it within the Labour Party, it's quite likely it
would never have happened at all. So he established almost immediately a style of leadership that was to become very familiar over
the next decade and more.

In many ways Blair's speech in 1994 was as significant as
Kinnock's in 1985, although less dramatic in its immediate impact
since it was only some hours after it was made that large numbers
of people in the party and the unions actually grasped what his
message was. It was so tentative that Clause IV, its chief subject,
was nowhere mentioned. But what took place in the years brack-
eted by those two leaders' speeches wasn't simply the demolition
of the old Labour Party and its replacement with an institution
designed in a more contemporary style. What happened was the
reallocation of the entire territory over which British political
conflict had been conducted for most of the twentieth century. It
erased the idea that there were certain interest groups that essentially belonged to the Conservatives and others that, most of the
time, would provide a Labour core vote.

It was the distancing of Labour from the unions that finally
eliminated the idea of it remaining essentially the party of the
working class – not least because it became increasingly difficult to

decide if something called the working class still existed and, if it did, what people might be contained within it. It was, after all, part of a social structure in which class was to a large extent defined by the nature of work. As manual work disappeared and definitions became more fluid, so the loyalties that had for so long been involved in questions of comparative social status became less binding. It was something that could be seen clearly in the way in which a new economic structure redefined the roles of women in their communities; for some people what that implied for relation-ships between women and men had, on at least one occasion as we'll see, explosive consequences.

The benefits for the Labour Party of this rebuilt identity have been obvious enough. The party has won three elections with majorities that, even at their lowest, have pushed the Opposition into the search for yet another leader and yet another set of policies which are both distinctive and somehow recapture the historical spirit of Conservatism. Making the poor work harder and giving lots more money to the rich being, at the time of writing, rather out of fashion, it's clear that finding a new line is a difficult trick in an age in which the other illusionist always seems to have your rabbit in his hat. It may be that the Tories will have to adopt some of the absolute certainties of the American neocons before they manage to seize the attention of a catatonic public. In the meantime the result of this long-term bafflement among the Tories about what they should do next has inevitably diminished the level of attention the parties can command among the voters and, increasingly, the non-voters. What is the argument at the heart of political life they ask, to which no coherent answer seems readily to hand.

Well, maybe that's not quite right, because one of the most compelling things about Tony Blair as a leader is the lengths to which he has gone to provoke disputes, not with the Opposition, but within his own party. The manner in which he set about the abolition of Clause IV set a pattern for his behaviour in office. Devolution, for example, or partial reform of the House of Lords are policies that happened fast and, consequently were at best incomplete. But because something has happened, because the system has been made different, however imperfectly, it will inevitably be further redrawn. University top-up fees, foundation hospitals and greater freedom for schools are among the policies that have infuriated people in his own party. You can't help feeling that here's a man who's looking for trouble. Even more so when it comes to things like identity cards and, above all, the war in Iraq, because of which Blair has been denounced in the most passionate terms by those who sit on the same side of the House of Commons. And all the while the Conservatives were digging deeper and deeper holes as they said, yes, they agreed with these policies or, on second thoughts, perhaps they didn't actually agree with them after all or, then again, perhaps they agreed with one of them and not the other. Or some of them more or less agreed or disagreed anyway.

The importance of this is that the main debate in British public life came, after 1997, to take place within the Labour Party rather than across the traditional party divide. It's what continues to make politics gripping and occasionally unpredictable, but it also removes the important decisions from the hands of the voters. Only to a very modest extent can you use the ballot box to support one bit of the Labour Party rather than another.

Oh well, it's sometimes argued, this is a temporary phenomenon in the long game of politics. Blair will be gone sooner rather than later and the ancient virtues of Labour will reassert themselves. Maybe, but don't hold your breath. It's interesting, for example, that the only two senior people to leave the government on a matter of principle in nine years were Clare Short and Robin Cook. And their principle was Iraq rather than any partisan disputes left over from the old days. In this, after all, they were standing shoulder to shoulder with Charles Kennedy and the Liberal Democrats.

But there's also the matter of Gordon Brown, a man who figures in the dreams of those who murmur the word socialism as they sleep restlessly. Perhaps, they think, he'll emerge to be some kind of young Lochinvar who will eventually sweep them back into the comforting certainties of the old days. Yet this is the Chancellor of the Exchequer who admires the American system of economic management more than any other. And he is the man, too, who has used tax credits to help people on low incomes rather than leaving it to union-led pay negotiations. Not only that, but he's sat year after year through all the policy decisions which have caused so much anguish to Blair's critics, someone whose economic say-so has often been essential to their implementation. It would take an act of breathtaking cynicism for him to turn round on the doorstep of 10 Downing Street and say that, actually, now you come to mention it, he had disagreed with most of them.

Now it would be very foolhardy indeed to say that we have reached a point in history where our political dispensation has been overturned for ever, that old-style party politics, notably the divisions between left and right, have been superseded by rather less galvanising arguments over what are essentially questions of management rather than principle. In the years since the war, a definitive outcome of this kind has been proclaimed with great regularity. In 1945 it was said that the Conservatives were finished; in 1959 Labour; in 1966 the Conservatives again; in 1983 Labour and in 2001, the Conservatives once more. There is an ebb and flow in political life in which the familiar seems eventually to reassert itself. Not entirely, though, as we can see from the persistence of what much of what the Thatcher government did, for example, and, as far as we can judge now, from the impact of New Labour. It's the case, too, that in the face of what looks like the permanent establishment of one set of ideas people look for other constitutional methods of getting a fresh purchase on power. In present circumstances they are likely to seem increasingly attractive.

VULGAR FACTIONS

IN THE RITUALS OBSERVED by worshippers at the what-might-have-been temple of Labour history, many flames are kept glimmering by those who blow on the embers of resentment and regret over events that took place a political lifetime ago and more. Ramsay MacDonald was never forgiven by his party for his decision to lead the National Government alongside the Conservatives and the Liberals in 1931. It became known as the great betrayal and even today, even in the minds of many people who were not born at the time, it is a party folk memory that helps sustain Labour's deep suspicion of coalition. When in 2006 the Commons marked the centenary of the founding of the Parliamentary Labour Party, Labour members hissed at the mention of MacDonald's name. It's also the case, as I've already mentioned, that the General Strike of 1926 was a powerful influence on the attitudes of the National Union of Mineworkers getting on for sixty years later.

In much the same way there are those who argue that the whole course of British political history might have turned on one event in 1970. That was Roy Jenkins's failure to cheer up the voters with a give-away Budget and so persuade enough of them to support Labour at the general election a couple of months later. Even by the simplistic standards of such alternative views of history you might say this doesn't stand up to a great deal of detailed scrutiny. At the same time it's certainly possible to argue that Jenkins's decision had a profound effect on the direction of the Labour Party for the next quarter of a century. Perhaps, too, the effect wasn't precisely the one that disappointed Labour supporters assumed at the time.

What happened in April 1970 was in any case pretty rare in that it arose from a politician taking an unusually high-minded view of the British public, their intelligence and their sense of propriety. In his autobiography, *A Life at the Centre*, Jenkins wrote about his reaction to "many people, both inside and outside the House of Commons, who would have looked for a bonanza. With an election pending, they regarded it as a certainty."

Jenkins himself was considerably more cautious, not least because he didn't think it would work in electoral terms. "I had sweated much too hard to turn the balance of payments... to be willing to put it all at risk by a give-away Budget, which in any case I regarded as a vulgar piece of economic management below the level of political sophistication of the British electorate."

That use of the word 'vulgar', which is not a common term of condemnation in contemporary politics, catches the essence of the popular image of Jenkins. Old Smoothiechops, as *Private Eye* called him, was seen as a fastidious man with refined tastes and patrician manner, redolent of the fine wines and expensive cigars of which he was a dedicated consumer. Not only did it annoy his critics that he ostentatiously enjoyed these things and gave a clear impression that he thought he deserved them, but he had also committed the worst class crime of all: he was a social climber who had abandoned his proletarian roots. And he had done so with indecent haste, virtually as soon as the doors of Balliol College, Oxford, had closed behind him in October 1938, when he was seventeen years old. The miner's son, the grammar school boy from the eastern valley of Monmouthshire, had overnight assumed the style of that alien race, the English upper middle class.

When, towards the end of the nineteen seventies, he was President of the European Commission, I greeted Jenkins at the entrance to the BBC in Cardiff where I was due to interview him. He was late. Well, I suggested tactfully, traffic was heavy at that time of the evening so no doubt his car had been held up in the rush.

"Oh no," he said, with the air of someone who normally travelled by Tardis. "You see, I had outwiders."

What? Outwiders? Oh, he means a motor cycle escort.

It was this aspect of Jenkins as much as his political views that drove some of his Labour colleagues mad with disapproval. That sense of superiority, the distance he maintained between himself and those who weren't his personal friends; the idea, persistently articulated in Wales, that somehow the way in which he'd reinvented himself was a betrayal of his past and an implied criticism of those who hadn't done the same. Speaking posh, swank, side, airs and graces even, sometimes, success, are considered to be detestable characteristics by quite sophisticated Welsh people who continue to exchange sniper fire from behind the crumbling barricades erected during the class war. They implied that Jenkins would have been able to speak perfectly normally if he'd chosen to do so but instead had adopted a mild impediment as some kind of foppish eighteenth-century affectation.

In his diary, Philip Weekes recorded a meeting with a group of Welsh MPs in January 1981. It was at the time of the foundation of the Social Democratic Party which made Jenkins, never warmly viewed by many of those colleagues, an even more unpopular figure. Philip wrote: "They all despised Jenkins and, as a Welshman, I felt they despised his accent above all else." In the conversation another South Wales politician complained: "Who ever met a genuine Welshman who couldn't pronounce his 'r's?" But in fact it's a very common defect among Welsh people, although it doesn't always take exactly the Jenkinsian form. It's not for nothing, for example, that the very distinguished the Welsh politician, John Morris (now Lord Morris of Aberavon KG) was often referred to privately by media people as John Movvis.

When taxed with the famous 'r' question on television, Jenkins looked embarrassed and mumbled about it. But elsewhere his explanation for the accent he had adopted perhaps revealed a sensitivity on the subject as he toyed with some cod phonetics. In *A Life at the Centre* he wrote: "I think there must be something in the air or the water of the Eastern Valley of Monmouthshire which washes away deviations from 'standard' English more easily than do those of most other localities. But they do not do so completely. I am told that to a Professor Higgins (or even to his most newly-joined assistant) my pronunciation of 'situation' is an immediate indication of Welsh origin."

Whatever the reason for the way in which he came to speak, Jenkins's acquisition of English polish and the distance he thus put between himself and his genuinely impressive Labour credentials, it gave rise to one of the most extraordinary statements I've ever heard about this aspect of public life. In Michael Cockerell's immensely diverting 1996 BBC film about Jenkins – *A Very Social Democrat* – Shirley Williams, a co-founder of the SDP, commented: "If he had gone on looking as if he had come from that Welsh valley I think his route to the premiership would have been unstoppable."

If we accept that analysis at face value then it seems that Roy

Jenkins must go down as the only British politician in history to have failed because he wasn't Welsh enough. Of course many Welsh people have made outstanding contributions to political life. Over the years they've led all three main parties. Lloyd George was one of the greatest statesmen of the twentieth century. Even Michael Howard called on his Llanelli origins when, in the 2005 election campaign, he said (only in Wales, you'll understand) that he wanted to become Britain's first Welsh-born prime minister. Nevertheless I don't believe these people or any others went round thinking, 'If only I'd made a bit more of the Welsh thing, I might have done really well'. More plausibly it seems likely that those who have succeeded have done so in spite of being Welsh.

In fact what Shirley Williams had to say is more revealing. Dedicated politicians are simply staggered when one of their number fails to make use of some natural advantage, particularly one of a sentimental nature, he or she has been handed on a plate. In Jenkins's case it wasn't just that he'd grown up in modest circumstances in a coal mining area, but that he had done so with the Labour equivalent of a silver spoon in his mouth.

His father, Arthur Jenkins, was an example of the determination and intelligence that in the coalfields often forced their way through to the front of the trade union and political queue. He was born in 1882, went into the mines at the age of twelve, and worked underground for most of the next twenty-four years. Like many talented people from the unions he got the chance of adult education, in his case at Ruskin College, Oxford. Like many others, too, he had an internationalist approach and, after Ruskin, spent three months in France. He went back to the pit but also began to establish a political career, on the Pontypool District Council in 1918, and then in 1919 on Monmouthshire County Council. He progressed in the miners' union as well, taking a senior job as a miners' agent. He became a member of the National Executive of the Labour Party.

So far, then, so typical of many people in the coal industry and other occupations who made their way by such routes to the heart of political power, in many cases as far as the Cabinet. But Arthur Jenkins also had a distinction given to few others. He went to gaol. And not only did he go to gaol but he did so for defending trade unionists; more than that, he did so during that most resonant of industrial conflicts, the General Strike. An ambitious socialist boy of the period might well have filled his letter to Father Christmas with a description of such a parent.

The incident that got Arthur Jenkins imprisoned took place in August 1926, well after the General Strike itself had ended but during the long, painful period when the miners stayed out alone. Men had gone to work at a small mine known as Quarry Level, between Crumlin and Pontypool. A mass picket, organised by Jenkins, went to the pit. The affair was reported by the *Western Mail* in its edition of August 31, 1926.

"A squad of police under Superintendent Spenlove drew their truncheons and charged 900 to 1000 miners, several of whom were injured. A deputation of Jenkins, Coldrick, Edwards and others, appointed at an earlier meeting to interview the 39 work-men who have returned to their employment on pre-stoppage terms and cards reported. The crowd of 200 booed when told by deputation that men refused to stop work. Stones were thrown; police already there; police attacked demonstrators with their batons. A crowd of women shouted at the police, 'You dirty swine,' 'You miserable cowards' etc.

"Mr Arthur Jenkins, the Miners' Agent, mounted a coal truck and shouted that the police had acted with terrible ferocity. He had seen an old man, who was sitting down peaceably, struck by a truncheon in the most wanton manner. Police reinforcements were rushed up from all parts of the county in motor cars and eventually the crowd dispersed."

It's impossible to read that report today without a sense of shock. It could have come from the *Western Mail* or the *Mirror* or the *Daily Telegraph* of almost sixty years later, even down to one, very different, Arthur standing in for another. Three months later, at the end of November, Arthur Jenkins was sent to prison for nine months for his part in this affair, an outcome that was to enhance his reputation in the district and the wider Labour Party.

Curiously, though, young Roy wasn't told about what had happened to his father. Since he was only just six when the sentence was passed it's perhaps not altogether surprising that he was kept in the dark. Arthur's absence was explained by the story that he was on an extended tour of coal mines in Germany. Some years were to pass before Roy became aware of exactly what had happened. Even then: "I picked up the story almost surrepti-tiously, through the chance remarks of others".

When Roy Jenkins became a prominent politician worldly people in the Labour Party used this as a stick with which to beat him and, ingeniously enough, they managed to find two entirely separate causes for criticism. One was that the truth had been kept from Jenkins because his family had been ashamed of what had happened. Leo Abse, later a successor of Arthur Jenkins's as MP for Pontypool, said the story had been concealed "not out of protectiveness but from sham respectability".

This arose, it was said, because of the superior social airs put on by Jenkins's mother, Hattie, whose father had been the general manager of an ironworks and so a rung or two up the class ladder. Abse wrote that the constituency had developed a distaste for Hattie Jenkins. "She was convicted of snobbery, a peccadillo elsewhere, but unfortunately a grave offence in the eastern valley of Monmouthshire... She seemed a silly woman but silly mothers assume the most extraordinary importance in the lives of even the most brilliant sons."

Jenkins was sufficiently stung by this assassination of his mother's character to respond directly to it in his autobiography, describing Abse as having made "a part-time occupation out of portraying my mother as a tremendously snobbish woman, alien to my father's beliefs and outlook on life, and a crucial influence on me".

Jenkins wrote that this was an inaccurate portrait drawn by someone who had met his mother only once. But, as he explained rather ruefully, it was an accusation that stuck as, down the years, one journalist after another, as journalists do, got out the files and copied this portrait of Mrs Jenkins into the various profiles and other articles written about her son. So opponents were confirmed in their view that not only was Jenkins a snob who was embarrassed about his background, but that snobbery also ran in the family.

At the same time, too, there were those who, like Shirley Williams, felt that Jenkins had failed to take proper political advantage of the hereditary kudos of being the son of a mining official who went to gaol in the General Strike. A different kind of politician would never have let the matter rest, but he seems to have avoided the subject. Given the style of speech and manner he'd adopted he might have been well aware that it would have sounded incongruous for someone like him to start banging on about the oppression of his working class father by the servants of the state acting as agents of rapacious capitalists. But, once again, there was also more than an element of fastidiousness about this reserve and, as it happened, that of his father.

He wrote: "Neither of us was remotely ashamed of what had occurred, or would have dreamed of denying it if the subject came up. Equally, however, neither of us wished to draw attention to it, to flaunt it as a special badge of virtue, or to make a *métier* out of being a victim (or the son of a victim) of a miscarriage of justice."

This is not to suggest that either Arthur Jenkins or Roy were above using their connections. After becoming MP for Pontypool in 1935 Arthur was made parliamentary private secretary to the Labour Leader, Clement Attlee, and, after the war, a junior minister in Attlee's government, resigning because of ill-health not long before his death in April 1946. Attlee became something of a patron of the young Roy and godfather to his first child. In 1946 he edited a volume of Attlee's speeches (and got paid by Attlee for doing so) and then wrote a biography of the Prime Minister. A clever young man anxious to make a career in politics could hardly have thought more carefully about how to begin. Even so, in the end there might have been something missing. He himself thought it was the ruthless steel needed to make the last yards into Downing Street. "I had slightly too many other interests," he said regretfully, long after his political career was at an end.

Those other interests, that lack of steel, might have accounted for the generous view he took of voters' likely attitudes in 1970 when composing a Budget out of tune with the expectations of many of his colleagues. Or a different kind of steel anyway, since it was hardly likely to be a popular thing to do. Much of the Cabinet's discussion of possible election dates revolved around the question of getting the 'right kind of Budget' although a large number of factors, many of them trivial to the eyes of people unschooled in ministerial neurosis, had to be taken into account.

In his diary entry for March 8, 1970, Richard Crossman records exchanges in which the Prime Minister, Harold Wilson, said that one of the problems in choosing an election date concerned the World Cup. England were the holders and it was due to be played in Mexico in June. "If it wasn't for that, he would favour the end of June, and was now trying to find out what time of day the match was played, because he felt this was a determining factor. Denis Healey was then asked his opinion and in a nutshell he firmly declared for the autumn unless we could manage the end of June. Fred Peart pointed out that we have never had a June election, and he thought we wanted late September or early October. Wedgy Benn said that with a reasonable Budget he would go for early June."

The Budget was clearly only one factor among many, but Jenkins's decision to cut income tax by only £200 million, rather than the £400 million that at one stage had been proposed, was certainly frugal. Jenkins identifies Crossman as one of those who wanted a give-away Budget but his reaction when a more cautious one was delivered was certainly not one of political panic. "I must admit," Crossman writes, "I fell asleep during Roy's Budget speech which was pretty heavy going, especially the international part."

In the end it's impossible to say how much influence Jenkins's cautiously correct approach – "correct, prim and proper" Crossman said of one aspect of it – had on the result of the June 18 election. Maybe it was more affected by Wakes Week, or the Coventry shut-down week, or the prospect of the cricket test matches being disrupted by demonstrations led by the anti-apartheid campaigner, Young Liberal and future Labour Cabinet Minister, Peter Hain. These were all among the considerations Wilson had raised with ministers when looking at dates. More likely, though, it was one of those bits of bad luck that lurk in the shadows waiting to mug unwary governments.

On June 15, three days before the polls opened, the trade figures for May were published showing a deficit of £31 million, a figure dramatically bad enough to cast doubt on the government's command of economic policy. It had been caused, it seemed, by an unexpected import cost – that of two jumbo jets. At this distance (where one hour's trade deficit would probably amount to £31 million) it seems an absurdly minor matter to influence anyone's vote. But the Wilson government had taken office in 1964 in the midst of an economic crisis and year after year the question of the balance of payments, left in a poor state by the Conservative Chancellor, Reginald Maudling, filled the headlines. It's hard to imagine now, but each month people would turn on the radio in grim anticipation of the latest trade figures, much as they might have listened to the news of battles during the Second World War.

While one set of figures by no means told the whole economic story, it was a reminder to voters of the severe pressures of the very recent past. After a long struggle the government had been forced to devalue the pound in 1967. After that it became enmeshed in an unpopular prices and incomes policy. That caused bad feeling among trade union members, while those who thought the unions too powerful had been dismayed by the decision the previous year to abandon *In Place of Strife*, and with it any attempt to introduce legislation to regulate labour relations. Wilson also blamed the warm weather during the campaign. Oh, and if those matters weren't quite enough, on the Sunday before the election England were defeated by Germany, ending their defence of that World Cup they had won in 1966.

One other explanation for the result offered at the time has a striking resonance now. Wilson might have liked to talk about Labour as being, in his phrase, the natural party of government, but others detected a shrugging of the shoulders among the electorate, a sense that perhaps it didn't matter all that much who actually won. That was reflected in the lowest turnout for a quarter of a century, even if the fact that 72 per cent of the electorate nevertheless voted illustrates how much more severe is the modern sense of disengagement with the political process.

If Labour had won in 1970 Roy Jenkins would almost certainly have been Foreign Secretary, as Wilson had promised, He might well have succeeded Wilson as Prime Minister, sooner rather than later. He was at least as enthusiastic about Europe as was Edward Heath, but whether he could have persuaded the Labour Party to support a British application for membership of the Common Market is more problematical. Maybe Britain wouldn't have joined at all at that stage. After a while the virtual road map becomes pretty well impossible to read. But it's also the case that the 1970 Budget, if indeed it did cost Labour the election, had a much more profound influence on the party's future direction.

It's something raised by David Marquand in a book of essays examining various aspects of Jenkins's career. Marquand is a former Labour MP who at one stage was political adviser to Roy Jenkins as President of the European Commission. He supports the view that to people on the left of the Labour Party the 1970 defeat was much more than simply another turn on the roundabout of political life. From 1951 until 1964 Labour had been out of office and it had returned to power carrying a huge weight of expectation of radical change. It didn't happen and the necessary economic growth, which was to be based on a new system of economic planning, didn't materialise.

Marquand wrote: "Thanks largely to Jenkins's stubborn resolution, the forced devaluation of 1967 had worked, but only after a long delay and at the cost of further spending cuts. Many hitherto moderate party members, as well as long-standing left-wingers, felt cheated. Before the election they had stifled their doubts. Now they began to suspect that the Left's explanation for what had gone wrong – that Wilson's ministers had been whoring after the false gods of the mixed economy, and betrayed their own people in the process – might have something in it."

The result was, Tony Benn was to write, that "the radicalisation of the Labour Party began from 1970. It wasn't just later. It began then." Or to put it another way, the origins of the civil war that was to consume the Labour Party a decade later lay in that election defeat, a defeat that might have been due to something as simple as Jenkins's failure to ease his Budget by another couple of hundred million pounds. So it was that, long before the convulsions of the eighties and nineties, Jenkins had actually had a crucial, if inadvertent, influence in the creation of New Labour. Such conclusions are tempting if, in the traditions of Miss Marple and Lord Peter Wimsey, amateur political detectives like to tease out a sensational denouement at the end of a notably tricky case. It won't wash, of course, except in so far as this was a conflict that eventually had to be resolved, but no one could have told you in 1970 what kind of course it might take over the next quarter of a century. The central, calamitous confrontation between Edward Heath and the miners that was, only a few years later, to alter so abruptly the country's political future couldn't have been predicted. But then, that wouldn't have happened at all if Labour had won that election.

*

From today's perspective I suppose most people would consider that Jenkins's chief contribution to British political life in the last thirty years of the twentieth century was much less to do with any supposed repercussions of his economic policy, although his Chancellorship is still widely admired, and much more with his key role in the country's entry into the Common Market, the consequences for him personally and, later, for the eventual direction of the Labour Party. His part in securing Britain's entry was an influential one and is recognised as such, but it was by no means as glorious as the reputation bestowed on it by the passage of time. It is the case that, on October 28, 1971, in the vote on the principle of entry he led 69 Labour rebels into the 'yes' lobby. The government got a majority of 112 and so the Labour vote in favour (plus 20 abstentions) might well have been decisive. But in all the detailed legislation that was to follow, Jenkins and the other Labour pro-Europeans voted against Heath and his administration. Sometimes it was only a tiny number of votes that kept the legislation from being entirely wrecked.

Jenkins's reasoning was that it was essential for him and his associates to maintain their positions within the Labour Party, of which he was then deputy leader. They could defy the Whip once and get away with it, but to vote against their own party's policy night after night would have been considered intolerable. In the not very long term this useful distinction didn't make very much difference. The Labour Party's anti-Europeans were not only in the majority but very much in command where it mattered. In 1972 they established it as party policy that a future Labour government would hold a referendum on membership of the market. Jenkins resigned as deputy leader and his prospects of ever being Prime Minister were destroyed, even though he made a last bid for the leadership when Wilson resigned in 1976.

What followed is a familiar enough story. Even before that leadership contest in 1976 Jenkins had been sounded out about becoming President of the European Commission. In the circumstances he was glad to take the job. But, as he contemplated Britain from the other side of the Channel, his thoughts become more and more occupied with the idea of a new political order in Britain, a need for what he described as "a strengthening of the radical centre." That was one of the phrases he used in the BBC's Dimbleby Lecture in November 1979 when he floated some of the ideas he had been developing in Brussels. He talked of coalition, a word which, as I say, has Labour traditionalists chewing the furniture. He also talked about the stimulus of the free market, the need to create wealth, caution in taxation policy and the need for the state "to know its place".

You certainly didn't need a copy of the *Junior Spy's First Book of Codes* to know what he was on about but, of course, it was a lecture that set out ideas and principles rather than any specific plan of action. Nevertheless, as Jenkins records in his autobiography, it prompted some people, in particular Shirley Williams and Bill Rodgers, to face at least the prospect of making a break with the Labour Party. The plan to do so came soon enough with the formation by the Gang of Four (Jenkins, Williams, Rodgers and David Owen) of the Council for Social Democracy and its intervention, in alliance with the Liberals, in the 1983 election.

That election, in which the Alliance got 25.4 per cent of the vote compared with Labour's 27.6 per cent, marked the moment when what you might call the realistic Labour left recognised that, after almost eighty years in the mainstream of British politics, their movement was in danger of dissolving into a rancorous sect. Neil Kinnock, the party's new leader, had not too long before had been an enthusiastic supporter of many of the policies being put forward by the Bennite left. In his time he was, for example, an anti-Common Market unilateralist of unquenchable zeal. But now he and others were pulled up sharply by a conclusion that has seized many politicians down the years: that clinging to peripheral ideological purity was no substitute for the ability to win political power through the ballot box.

There's no question that the formation of the SDP under the leadership of Jenkins and the other members of the Gang of Four, followed by the defection of twenty-two other Labour MPs (and one Tory), had a vital, perhaps decisive, influence on the nature of the Labour Party. Indeed, so influential was its limited life that the SDP's demise turned out to be contained in its origins. In the end many of its principles could be seen in the policies of New Labour as contained in the philosophy expounded by Tony Blair. It would be wrong to say that New Labour equals old (defunct) SDP but it's still the case that Roy Jenkins was an admirer of, and important counsellor to, Tony Blair. And that relationship thus provides a powerful connection to one of the mainstream traditions of the old Labour Party. Throughout much of the party's existence internal disputes have been an indispensable element of its character, and remain so. On that basis it's impossible to dismiss Jenkins as some kind of outsider.

In this light you might consider that his most significant contribution to the development of British politics in the late twentieth century was as a catalyst for some of the most important changes that were to re-shape the system. After all, it's the question of Europe that has been the one of the central elements in the paralysis that has seized the Conservative Party, as well as its inability to grasp the ideas and, more important, the people that might revive it as a credible organisation and opposition. Jenkins (and Ted Heath, of course) can claim at least a share of the credit for that, as he can at least indirectly for the creation of a kind of Labour Party that has enjoyed a dominance over modern British political life which in the previous half century had been exercised for any extended period only by the Conservatives.

★

There is another area of modern life in which Jenkins's influence can be seen at its most radical. And there are plenty of people who, reminded of his record, consider it to be the most deplorable aspect of his long years in public life. He was influential in and typical of a social transformation that gripped British society, something so that went so deep that people have almost forgotten about the atmosphere and practices of less than half a century ago. It was well beyond and more lasting than the temporary rise and fall of political parties and the different emphasis they put on familiar areas of policy as they sought the attention and approval of restless voters. It was summed up in perhaps the single most arresting question asked in a courtroom in the second half of the twentieth century.

At the Old Bailey in October 1960 Mervyn Griffith-Jones, prosecuting counsel, asked a jury at the Old Bailey: "Is it a book you would wish your wife or your servants to read?"

The book, of course, was *Lady Chatterley's Lover*, and in a single phrase Griffith-Jones had revealed the gulf that had grown up between what many people thought the world was like and what it had actually become. Servants had disappeared from all but the most wealthy homes; even in 1960 men would have been increasingly reluctant to lay down what kind of books their wives should and should not read. Within a year of the jury giving Griffith-Jones a dusty answer on this matter, two million copies had been sold in Britain.

And less than three years after that, in a different court case, someone else with a double-barrelled Welsh name encapsulated the age with another rhetorical question. It happened in June 1963 at the trial of Stephen Ward, one of the central public events in the great sensations of the Profumo Affair. A barrister told a witness, Mandy Rice-Davies, that Lord Astor had denied her allegations of unseemly sexual behaviour at his house parties at Cliveden. Her reply ensured her the immortality of the dictionaries of quotations. "He would, wouldn't he?"

It seems to me that those two brief interventions are in themselves enough to illuminate vividly the spirit of the age. The first was the anachronistic effort of a failing paternalism to restrict people's freedom to decide what were essentially matters for individual judgement: what they could and could not read and, soon enough, how they should conduct their private lives. The second was the public expression of the view, which is now common currency, that people in positions of power and privilege not only tell lies sometimes, but probably do so as a matter of course. Many years on there is a school of thought that still insists that much of what is bad in modern society stems from such outbreaks of disrespect and what they represented.

For this state of affairs Roy Jenkins has to take some of the blame or, you might say, credit. He had, as a backbencher, led the campaign for to rewrite the law on obscenity. It took from 1954 until 1959 to get the Obscene Publications Bill on to the statute book. The new law meant that for the first time the question of the artistic merit of a book could be used in its defence. So thirty-five witnesses, including clergymen and some of the most distinguished literary critics of the day, turned up at the Old Bailey to speak for Lady Chatterley. She was acquitted and the British public was at last free to read words that today are routinely used in some of the more upmarket newspapers, a well as in the cinema and on the television.

Jenkins was certainly influential in these developments but it's clear that such apparently dramatic movements don't come about because of the momentum provided by an individual, however determined, but because he has articulated a much wider consensus for a more liberal approach. It was significant, for instance, that in the case of the Obscene Publications Bill he got the help of the Conservative Home Secretary, R.A. Butler. And in his turn he was to do the same for other reformers during his first period of Home Secretary from 1967 to 1969.

Although maintaining the official government stance of neutrality he spoke in support of David Steel's private member's bill on abortion, making parliamentary time available for it, as well as for Leo Abse's legislation to reform the law on homosexuality. There were other ways in which he intervened more directly to modernise the system. It gives you a jolt to realise, for example, not so much that Jenkins ended the flogging of prisoners but that the practice had persisted for long into the modern era. To this day his is one of the names reached for by critics who believe that what they saw as the precipitous decline of Britain was owed to the kind of liberalising measures taken in this period. There are even those who think the resumption of a certain amount of flogging would resolve a number of problems. To them he is the guilty man who more or less invented the permissive society.

That wasn't a term he cared for. He explained on one occasion: "A better phrase is the civilised society, a society based on the belief that different individuals will wish to make different decisions about their pattern of behaviours, and that, provided these do not restrict the freedom of others, they should be allowed to do so within a framework of understanding and tolerance".

In such issues at that time it looks as though the House of Commons (or enough of it to cobble the requisite majorities together) was often in advance of public opinion when it came to social liberalism. It's not surprising to find Jenkins in that company because, although his main occupation for a large part of his life was politics (he fought his first election at the age of twenty-four and became an MP at twenty-seven) he had a parallel career as a prolific and accomplished author, especially of political biography. He wrote twenty books during his life; at the age of 75 he won the Whitbread biography prize. When he was 80, his biography of Churchill was published to wide acclaim. In a modern politician such industry in another cause often provides grounds for suspicion. Harold Wilson used to suggest that he was lazy, by which he meant that Jenkins didn't stay in his office late enough at night, but the charge is clearly absurd.

Those who saw him at the beginning of the SDP campaigns, when he was in his early sixties, couldn't doubt his commitment to the mechanics of politics either. When he fought the Warrington by-election in 1981 he was a man who, as President of the European Commission, had not long before been carried round as if he were a year's wages at ICI, outwiders and all. Now he had to get back on the streets in the most cheeringly democratic part of political life which obliges all candidates, however grand, to make direct physical contact with the electorate. In the brief time I was there I never saw him kiss a baby, but if one had been offered he would undoubtedly have done so. At such times Jenkins, who had something of an obsession with numbers (he took a keen interest in railway timetables), would carry a clicker in his pocket which he pressed to record the exact numbers of people he'd met in the course of the campaign. At Glasgow Hillhead, which he won in the following year, the final total on the clicker was five thousand.

Such minor eccentricities weren't known to the general public and whether they would have loved him any the better for them it's impossible to say. Perhaps they would have tempered the old Smoothiechops image, but there was another matter that was even more unexpected. That was his taste for the company of upper-class women, not for the social cachet they might bring as congenial lunch or dinner companions, but as lovers.

In an age of indiscretion it's difficult to think of any sexual revelation about a public figure in recent times that would make you pause for more than a few moments as you turned the pages of your newspaper. The exposure of the liaison between John Major and Edwina Currie might have been the exception to that general rule; some Liberal Democrats have made us pay more attention occasionally. But what we now know about, say, the royal family means we understand there is no area of society that is above taking part in the non-stop bonking Olympics that is the chief sporting interest of the British press. Even so, when I watched Michael Cockerell's film about Roy Jenkins, there came one of those moments when you leap forward to turn the sound up a few notches. Cockerell's commentary suddenly told us that among Jenkins's recreations was a series of love affairs with glamorous and aristocratic women, including Jackie Kennedy's sister, Princess (or ex-Princess) Lee Radziwill, as well as the wives of various friends. Had someone switched channels while my attention was elsewhere? This was supposed to be a programme about Roy Jenkins, for goodness' sake.

But indeed it was. What did Jenkins have to say about all this, Cockerell wanted to know.

"I've never commented on these things," he drawled, only just perceptibly opening his mouth as he spoke, looking like a bad ventriloquist. "I think that if you deny something it is ungallant and if you confirm something... it's like Budget secrets, much better not talked about."

During this interview Jenkins looked, I thought, a little uncomfortable, but was it also possible to see on his face a faint flickering of remembered pleasure? "I've never done anything I'm ashamed of," he said.

But, Cockerell persisted, wasn't he worried that if people found out he might be forced to resign? Jenkins's response was dismissive. "I've never been worried about having to resign on a matter of that sort."

Even so, you can't help wondering what might have happened if details of one of Jenkins's affairs had suddenly become public. Even if he hadn't been driven from office by the endless phoney moralising of the *Daily Mail* and others ("A man who would lie to his wife might also lie to the country," is the ritual condemnation on such occasions, despite the fact that it makes no logical sense) his political authority would surely have taken a substantial hit, if only from the sheer noise that accompanies such sensations. If Jenkins had been a younger man, and the peak of his career had occurred twenty years later, surely there would have been every prospect that it would have been cut short by sexual scandal.

Except for one thing. The most sensational exposures of recent years have more often than not emerged from the public statements of vengeful or greedy partners, a group that most famously includes the late Diana, Princess of Wales. In contrast to the conventions of modern manners, Jenkins's affairs were with people who kissed and didn't tell, or at least didn't tell reporters. In the story of these adventures it's frequently said that relationships between all those involved, including his wife, Jennifer, remained undamaged by what went on. Whatever the moral aspects of this conduct might have been there's no doubt that it conformed exactly to Jenkins's definition of the civilised society.

And despite the hysterical condemnation that often pursues adulterous politicians, the atmosphere of public life in Britain has moved a long way in the direction that, in office and out of it, Jenkins encouraged, facilitated and endorsed. Where, not all that long ago, homosexual politicians might have feared the consequences of exposure, gay cabinet ministers now speak openly about their sexual orientation. They are usually brought down by what they keep secret rather than what they admit. You might say that in many ways the Jenkins view of life has prevailed, except in regard to Europe, which remains an unresolved dilemma at the heart of political life. It's an interesting footnote, by the way, that, when he was President of the European Commission, Jenkins was instrumental in the creation of the European Monetary System, something that, in the 1990s, was to wreck the Conservative Party as a political force, at least in the medium term.

★

Well, perhaps we are now all social democrats in most respects, or those who run things are anyway. The central question is whether this is a permanent state of affairs or simply one of those phases through which Britain has passed as one set of ideas or another has prevailed for a brief period before being supplanted by another set. It wasn't very long, after all, from the Attlee Government's avalanche of public ownership to the torrent of privatisation under Margaret Thatcher, scarcely half a lifetime. It'll all be different under the next guy, the resistance tell each other, or maybe under the one after that. And one place they look for their inspiration is to someone else who climbed out of the South Wales coalfield to set an example that was more flamboyant, and perhaps more enduring, than anything achieved by Roy Jenkins.

In July 1971, divisions within the Labour Party over the Common Market had boiled over into heated meetings and personal confrontations. In public, Jenkins, as deputy leader, was unable to speak in favour of entry. But at a meeting of the parliamentary party he was free to say what he thought, something that included powerful attacks on Harold Wilson and Jim Callaghan. In an encounter later that evening, Richard Crossman made an unexpected criticism, comparing him with Aneurin Bevan.

"You have all the Welsh capacity for wrecking," Crossman said. "But maddeningly for the rest of us you are a Bevan with the big difference that you have the press and the establishment on your side."

At first sight this seems an absurd comparison to make. Apart from an accident of geography there could hardly have been two men in the same country, never mind the same party, who could have been more different. But then you realise the Crossman was on to something. Bevan and Jenkins actually had so much in common that they might have been mirror images of each other. Bevan, another man with a slight speech impediment, was also the son of a Monmouthshire miner (and a miner himself) who came to enjoy the company and patronage of the rich and influential. He was sometimes described as a natural aristocrat because of his confidence in his own abilities and his taste for good living; for such reasons he was mocked by Brendan Bracken, a Tory minister and a friend, as a "Bollinger bolshevik".

Both men were at the heart of divisions within the Labour Party. Jenkins resigned as deputy leader over the question of Europe, Bevan more spectacularly as Minister of Labour in 1951 over the issue of health service charges. Jenkins and Bevan were also exceptionally able ministers, Jenkins at the Home Office and the Treasury, Bevan as the man who was responsible for the one great enduring creation of the 1945 government, the National Health Service. The mirror image comes from their very different positions in their party. Jenkins was on the right wing, Bevan the insurrectionist of the left, for years at the heart of Labour's sour internal divisions. Yet of all people it was Bevan who was to shatter the cherished dreams of the left and leave his friends and acolytes in horrified disarray.

He did so in one of the most famous political speeches of modern times, one that has reverberated down the years because of its vivid language, its huge emotional charge, the sense of momentous events it contained. Even now, despite the imperfections of the recording systems of half a century ago, you still catch your breath when you hear the sound of old friendships and allegiances being ripped apart.

It was in Brighton on October 4, 1957, that Bevan, Shadow Foreign Secretary, rose at the Labour Party's annual conference to speak on the question of unilateral nuclear disarmament, specifically on a motion that called on the party to renounce the testing or manufacture of nuclear weapons in any form whatsoever. Long after Bevan was dead it remained one of the defining aspirations of the left. For him to oppose it, as he did, was a slap in the face of those who saw him as their leader, who were proud to call themselves Bevanites.

It entered history, of course, as he tore into what he saw as the flawed reasoning of those who supported unilateralism. Sending a British Foreign Secretary "naked into the conference chamber" is even today as familiar as a proverb. And later, the most stinging phrase of all: "You call that statesmanship. I call it an emotional spasm."

Among those who felt the lash was Bevan's close friend, Michael Foot, who wrote later: "At that moment, as the words indicate, he was caught in a frontal clash with a great section of the audience, and if many had not been nearer to tears, the whole place might have broken into uproar." Foot also wrote of the aftermath of this event: "The Left of the Party looked for a moment as if it had exterminated itself. Without its incomparable leader it was unlikely to gather strength for years."

Apologists for Bevan claim that he was to a great extent misunderstood and certainly misrepresented over this speech. He wasn't arguing in favour of nuclear weapons as a deterrent, but over two other central issues. One was the question of abandoning, without debate or consultation with the other countries concerned, the international alliances Britain had entered into. The second was the moral impossibility, as he saw it, of Britain repudiating the Bomb but at the same time entering into alliances with countries that retained it; not having the Bomb but being protected by it nonetheless. On the night before he made the speech he said, as Michael Foot recorded in his biography: "I do not regard loyalty to parties as the first of all loyalties. There are other supreme loyalties."

In one sense, though, the Brighton speech was a striking contribution to Labour Party unity. It marked the stage at which the Welsh wrecker became the Welsh healer. Or up to a point, anyway, since he had pretty well wrecked his own faction and given comfort to the man they liked least of all, the Labour leader, Hugh Gaitskell, someone described by Bevan years before as a desiccated calculating machine. But two years later Bevan not only appeared as an important ally of Gaitskell's but he also established himself as a pivotal figure in the party leadership.

In 1959 Labour lost its third successive general election. The Conservatives, under Harold Macmillan had a majority of 100 and some commentators were writing Labour off for good. At the postponed party conference in November of that year Labour turned, as it often did in such circumstances, to the question of its core beliefs, specifically public ownership. Barbara Castle began the argument, using her chairman's speech to launch a vigorous defence of the principle. Later, Gaitskell took a different line, not opposing nationalisation as such but nevertheless saying that, after forty years, the party constitution, which embodied the idea in Clause IV, should perhaps be brought up to date. Bevan, who had become deputy leader, bridged the ideological divide. In their speeches, he said, both Castle and Gaitskell had quoted him. Therefore, he argued, quoting Euclid, "if two things are equal to a third thing they are equal to each other". Or to put it another way, Castle and Gaitskell must agree with each other since they both agreed with him, Bevan.

This piece of rhetorical sleight-of-hand allowed him to talk about what should unite the party rather than what divided it. He launched a fierce attack on the affluent society, an ugly society, a meretricious society. It was, he said, using that word chosen some years later by Roy Jenkins, "a vulgar society".

There was much more of what Michael Foot described as perhaps one of the three or four greatest speeches Bevan had ever delivered. He had saved Gaitskell and the party from the consequences of a damaging split and in so doing he had greatly advanced his own authority and reputation. Roy Jenkins wrote briefly of it that the conference was "a near disaster for Gaitskell and left Bevan for the first time in a commanding position with the centre of the party".

What might eventually have been the consequences of this new alignment, you're bound to wonder. Would Bevan, one way or another, have supplanted Gaitskell? And there is no answer. It was Bevan's last speech. Eight months later he was dead. And by the time of the next election so was Gaitskell. Perhaps there was a clue in what Bevan said to Michael Foot in the last months of his life, as he lay in hospital before an operation for cancer. "He gave me a genial dissertation, half-warning, half-lament, on how nothing could be achieved outside the Party: 'never underestimate the passion for unity and don't forget it's the decent instinct of people who want to do something.'"

Between the two of them, Jenkins and Bevan, they embrace all the most pressing concerns of Labour politics of the twentieth century. Their similarities are as striking as their differences, the two miners' sons from Monmouthshire who took such different routes to the top of the same party and who influenced it in such distinctive ways. What's perhaps most curious of all is that it should have been Bevan, the perpetual rebel, whose last major public political act should have been to try to heal divisions; and that in contrast it was Jenkins, who had made himself the smooth establishment figure, the diplomat, who broke with his party and in the process contributed substantially to its reinvention in a different form, just as he had reinvented himself all those years previously.

He might never be entirely forgiven for that, for being the Bevan of the right, while Bevan himself, despite the blows he had rained on his own adherents over nuclear weapons, remains a heroic figure whose memory is called upon by anyone seeking a cheap round of applause. He never forgot where he came from or what he had been, his disciples say. His monument, the National Health Service, is portrayed as a mighty tribute to the care of the struggling class of people from which he had emerged. His example continues to have an almost biblical authority, but as in the case of religion, the further we get away from the events themselves the easier it is to quarrel over the significance they have today.

OUR PEOPLE

In January 1946, Aneurin Bevan found himself at the centre of a great public scandal. Not because of what he said, which was his usual way of getting into trouble, but because of what he did. Or, rather, what he didn't do. It was then he became, according to Michael Foot, the first man in history to attend a royal banquet at St James's Palace in a navy blue suit.

"Bevan had never worn a dinner jacket in his life," Foot wrote, "and since he regarded it as the livery of the ruling class he did not want to start. Must he spend precious clothing coupons or resort to Moss Bros for the purpose of making himself look foolish? This would be for him the acme of vulgarity – another of his favourite words. He resolved to set a new fashion or rather sustain the old fashion of the Wales of his youth. Of course the newspapers made a sensation of it, but at the banquet itself hardly an eyebrow was raised."

Bevan's wife, Jennie Lee, recorded in her own memoir that for the occasion Bevan wore "a well-fitting dark suit, an immaculate white shirt and a light-grey silk tie". But, she wrote, the next day the press reported "the important news that he had turned up at the Palace wearing a blue suit and brown boots (brown boots, I ask you) the purpose being to convey the impression that he had been deliberately uncouth and discourteous to the Queen."

Ah well, you might think, that was one of those battles that people fought long ago, a minor act of subversion, just as schoolboy republicans rushed from the cinema at the end of the main picture to avoid having to stand for the national anthem. It was a time, after all, when a working man would own, at most, one suit, and possession of a dinner jacket (or even the money to hire one) was the badge of considerable affluence. For Bevan to have worn such a costume might indeed have seemed to him a treacherous act, like putting on the uniform of the opposing army in the class war.

But even on that basis Bevan clearly didn't think this was a matter of more than minor symbolism. The Prime Minister,

Clement Attlee, was deeply upset by the incident and Bevan, in Michael Foot's words, came to the conclusion "that it was not worth mounting the barricades for a suit". He bought a dinner jacket – or at least Jennie Lee went to a shop get one for him. But when Mrs Attlee told Jennie how pleased she was at this turn of events and how much she was looking forward to seeing Bevan in his new outfit, it was all too much. The jacket remained in a cupboard, unworn. The sneers of his opponents were no problem; it was the patronising approval of his own side he couldn't take, something that happens in politics more often than you might think.

Old-fashioned though such a controversy seems now, for many years afterwards questions of dress served as a method of conducting public debate in the guise of a fashion commentary on the political catwalk. So Bevan's transgression was a minor matter alongside the affair of Michael Foot and the donkey jacket. More accurately, donkey jacket is what the press called the coat he was wearing in November 1982 when, as Leader of the Opposition, he laid a wreath at the Cenotaph on Remembrance Sunday.

"It wasn't a donkey jacket," he was saying twenty years later when journalists were still asking him about it. "It was a perfectly respectable dark green coat." And he added: "The Queen Mother said she liked it very much".

But the newspapers accused him of insulting the memory of British troops, of not paying sufficient respect. One implication, not very subtly made, was that Foot was a man of personally shambolic habits that made him unfit to run the country. But the subtext was, we all understood, that Foot was an old leftie, a unilateralist, maybe even a pacifist, which he never was, a republican, a subversive, someone, to be frank, who was not to be trusted in matters that went to the heart of patriotism. Such ideas, largely unspoken, were entirely preposterous. It's difficult to think of anyone more patriotic than Foot. On another occasion the *Sunday Times* went further and was more specific. Foot, it claimed, had been a KGB agent. Even when he was ninety years old you couldn't miss the satisfaction in his voice as, at his home in Hampstead, he showed you round the expensive kitchen paid for by his successful libel action against the newspaper.

As late as the twenty-first century, I suppose, the so-called donkey jacket affair would raise a lot of hostility. After all, the fact that Peter Sissons wore a dark red tie rather than a black one when he read the news on the evening of the Queen Mother's death was taken by many newspapers as incontrovertible evidence of the BBC's contempt for the monarchy and, by extension, everything else that had long made Britain great. But Bevan's 1946 gesture would seem positively quaint in a world in which distinctions of dress have largely disappeared, where scruffiness, especially designer scruffiness, is much prized among the wealthy and the influential. A few days stubble and a drab suit that looks as though it's just been pulled out from under the bed are the sure signs of social confidence. These are people to whom possession of a traditional dinner jacket would be considered to be, at best, an indication of a lack of aspiration as well as of a shortage of cash.

Interestingly, the only man who kept the argument going was Gordon Brown who, half a century after Bevan had made much of Fleet Street swoon at his flamboyant disrespect, ignored the black tie conventions of the occasion when he made the first of his annual speeches as Chancellor of the Exchequer at the Mansion House. He was still doing the same thing as late as 2005, when one reporter described the Chancellor's tie as looking as if it had been used as a bib by his young son. Now, though, you wonder what the message is. Somehow it looks like an expression of solidarity with a class of people that no longer exists, a way of behaving that's no more revolutionary than Tony Blair's occasional middle-class dad appearances – in his shirt sleeves and carrying a mug of tea – before the cameras in Downing Street.

If Gordon Brown's refusal to wear a dinner jacket in the twenty-first century seemed to be a puzzling act of minor rebellion, when Bevan did the same thing his message was clear enough: that there were two broad classes of people and you could distinguish one from the other to a large extent by what they wore. More than that, under those clothes there was a conflict between those Bevan called our people, people who were essentially virtuous and wise but oppressed, and the others, who were shallow, greedy and self-interested. In his last great speech, to the Labour conference in 1959, he saw this distinction as being a cause for optimism.

"I have enough faith in my fellow creatures in Great Britain to believe that when they have got over the delirium of the television, when they realise that their new homes that they have been put into are mortgaged to the hilt, when they realise that the moneylender has been elevated to the highest position in the land, when they realise that the refinements for which they should look are not there, that it is a vulgar society of which no decent person could be proud, when they realise all those things, when the years go by and they see the challenge of modern society not being met by the Tories who can consolidate their political powers only on the basis of national mediocrity, who are unable to exploit the resources of their scientists because they are prevented by the greed of capitalism from doing so, when they realise that the flower of our youth goes abroad today because they are not being given opportunities of using their skill and their knowledge properly at home, when they realise all the tides of history are flowing in our direction, that we are not beaten, that we represent the future: then, when we say it and mean it, then we shall lead our people to where they deserve to be led."

Not the least extraordinary thing about that passage is that it was delivered as a single sentence, 220 words long (or at any rate that is how it's reproduced in Michael Foot's book) but still makes sense. It's even more striking because of its lofty account of the intelligence and maturity of the average voter. But above all what makes it arresting is that, as a piece of political soothsaying, it is totally and completely wrong. The delirium of television, the homes mortgaged to the hilt, the central place of the moneylender in most people's lives, in short that vulgar society Bevan deplored so much, are all aspects of life considered indispensable to a civilised existence in modern Britain. Far from turning their backs on such seductions, the man and woman in the street pursued them tirelessly across the succeeding decades and on into the twenty-first century. The world that Bevan believed in 1959 could be retrieved once more was slipping further into oblivion even as he extolled its virtues.

It's possible to see now that Bevan's death was one of those milestones we can use to measure the distance between the familiar conflicts of class-based politics and the more diffuse approach that came to characterise public debate in the following decades. It was a period when the arguments ceased to be about quality and concentrated instead on quantity. If one saying above all others marked the extent of that then it was Harold Macmillan's statement in 1957: "Let us be frank about it: most of our people have never had it so good". Macmillan was mocked for speaking in a way that was considered to expose the complacency of his government and the poverty of its ambition, but Bevan's conference speech two years later underlined the accuracy with which the Conservative Prime Minister had indeed caught the mood of the times. Bevan thought it could change back, but it didn't.

This is perhaps one of the central reasons why Bevan continues to exert such a hold on the imagination of those who struggle against the limitations of what has become, in the UK, essentially a post-political world in which having it so good has become the main driver of policy, a world in which it is increasingly difficult to distinguish (in Bevan's words) "the delirium of television" from the reality of everyday life. After all, one of the most influential cultural developments of modern times has been the emergence of something called reality television. This is despite the fact that television can never be anything but television, even at its most profound only an intimation of reality.

Perhaps above all, though, the most substantial alteration in the character of British society has been brought about by the disappearance of the group that could be described, notably by the left, as *our people*. At the end of the fifties it was clear enough who they were. They worked in coalmines, shipyards, factories, steelworks, quarries and on the railways; in many cases they lived side by side in communities that were defined by their industries; they had a common understanding of their distinctive existence that could be grasped only imperfectly by outsiders. In the succeeding years the nature of work has for most people been utterly transformed; the great industries have been almost entirely erased from the landscape; there are now more television producers than coal miners in South Wales, for example, and more often than not next door neighbours have little idea of the nature of each other's working lives.

The homage that is still paid to Bevan is, I think, a way of maintaining a connection with this past existence, a time when the answers to pressing economic and social questions seemed simpler than they do today; above all the idea that the condition of working people might be most readily improved by the direct exercise of the power of government. Bevan articulated this idea on their behalf with great authority and magnetism. But his death in the summer of 1960 coincided with the onset of a revolution in the social character of Britain (including, of course, those first stirrings of the permissive society energetically assisted by Roy Jenkins) which, in his speech only a few months before, Bevan had rejected as being unworthy of the people represented by the

Labour Party. The fact that he died at what we can now see was the beginning of the end of a political era paradoxically persuades his admirers that his views have more rather than less weight in contemporary life. He represents some kind of golden age, utopian in aspiration if not in achievement, no less idyllic, if no more real, than John Major's Britain of "long shadows on county grounds, warm beer, invincible green suburbs, dog lovers and... old maids bicycling to Holy Communion through the morning mist".

There is, though, one crucial principle expounded by Bevan that modern politicians might usefully keep at the forefront of their minds. In the second paragraph of his only book, *In Place of Fear*, he wrote of the central question which had been, to young workers like himself, "a burning, luminous mark of interrogation. Where was power and which the road to it?" The answer to that question wasn't as simple as you might think. In a speech to the House of Commons in 1943, he described a conversation in which his father had told him that the local council was a very important place indeed and that the councillors were very important men.

"When I got older I said to myself: 'The place to get to is the Council. That's where the power is.' So I worked very hard and, in association with my fellows, when I was about twenty years of age, I got on the Council. I discovered when I got there that the power had been there, but it had just gone. So I made some enquiries, being an earnest student of social affairs, and I learned that the power had slipped down to the County Council. That was where it was and where it had gone to. So I worked very hard again and I got there and it had gone from there too."

The source of power remains as elusive today and the search for it just as challenging to young men and women who want to make things different. In theory it lies in the House of Commons, and that is true to the extent that, in the last resort, members of parliament can drive a government from office. Such a thing occurs rarely and only when a government has, as in 1979, either a very narrow majority or no majority at all. That might arise again in due course, but the era of landslides or near landslides, almost unbroken from 1983 onwards, has reduced the influence of individual MPs and the authority of parliament itself. Apart, that is, from the Major era when Tory backbenchers kicked their own government to the point of death: where does power lie, they might have been asking then, and how can we give it to someone else? That was followed by the long period in which the Conservatives failed to identify the people or the measures that would make them a serious opposition, and so emerged the conditions in which power in practice passed pretty well entirely to the executive. The significance of this state of affairs, combined with the convergence of policy between the two main parties, wasn't wasted on the voters who decided in increasing numbers that general elections didn't make a great difference to anything very much. Certainly many didn't find them compelling enough to make it worth missing the football or *Emmerdale* for the opportunity to put a cross on a ballot paper.

That's not to say that people weren't interested in matters which were more broadly political; animal welfare, say, globalisation, Iraq, organic food, the environment. It's just that they were unable to find a way of translating such concerns into support for any of the mainstream political parties. The question became whether they might seek other ways, apart from the march or the demonstration, of by-passing parliament and achieving political influence through other forums.

★

To suggest that the United Kingdom's newish devolved assemblies might provide the arena in which some form of renewed enthusiasm for the political process might be cultivated is to risk provoking derision. The best advice might be to check the cat to see if it's laughing. After seven years, the Scottish Parliament is most famous for completing a new parliament building at a cost of more than £400 million – ten times the original estimate. In the rest of the UK the most admired achievement of the National Assembly for Wales is the provision of free bus travel for pensioners. So gripped are the populations of these countries by this rolling out of democracy that in 2003 fewer than half the people of Scotland bothered to vote (a drop of almost 10 per cent from the first election in 1999) while only 38 per cent of the people of Wales remembered to do the same, a reduction of nine per cent over the same period.

But then, the fact that the Welsh Assembly exists at all is down to yet another run of chance at the gaming tables where the turn of a single card might have sent the disconsolate punter empty-handed out of the political casino. For example, even a minor incident could have swallowed up the majority of 6,721 out of a million votes cast by only 50 per cent of the electorate in the 1997 devolution referendum. The last dramatic gasp of the event came in the early hours of September 19 when, in the final declaration, Carmarthenshire turned in a big enough Yes majority to swing the whole result. A prolonged thunderstorm on the previous evening might have been all that was needed to keep a small but decisive number of voters at home.

Then again, who can now assess the impact of the death of Princess Diana and the week's moratorium on campaigning that followed it. The Princess was very popular in Wales, particularly when she turned up at rugby matches with her sons. The Prince of Wales, on the other hand, was not much admired and was often portrayed as the chilly, not to mention adulterous, representative of an alien, undemocratic authority. Might some people have thought that a vote for devolution was a posthumous vote for poor, abandoned Di?

Or there's the analysis of the former Plaid Cymru president, Dafydd Wigley, who has suggested that William Hague's decision to marry Ffion Jenkins could have made all the difference. His thesis is that the impeccably Welsh Miss Jenkins was a devolution enthusiast and that, in deference to her views, her besotted fiancé, then Leader of the Opposition, appeared in Wales only once during the campaign, despite the fact that, as a former Welsh Secretary, he might have been expected to carry considerable weight on the issue. (The Welsh Office was also where love had blossomed between William and Ffion.) Well, maybe, although we're unlikely ever to know the truth. And in any case, given William Hague's subsequent campaigning record, it's possible that further interventions from him might actually have increased the size of the pro-devolution majority.

The central point about all this speculation is to illustrate once again the fact that significant outcomes can hang on small events. If fewer than four thousand people had voted No instead of Yes there wouldn't have been an assembly in 1999. I suspect, however, that there would have been one eventually, if only in response to the miasma of discontent that would have enveloped Wales as people who had rejected devolution discovered, when deprived of it, that they had actually been in favour of it all along. The subsequent grizzling, an occupation in which Welsh politicians are undisputed world leaders, would have been insupportable.

In UK terms, the creation of a Scottish Parliament and, even more so, a Welsh Assembly, were seen as being in themselves small events. And of course they were, in that people's lives in those two countries were not noticeably altered while the English, apart from their habitual suspicion and resentment that Scotland and Wales might be getting an unfair share of public cash, didn't really see what it had to do with them. A few metropolitan journalists dropped by when someone famous – the Queen, Tony Blair – was in town, scoffed for a while, and went home again. But they had missed the point. Maybe we all had.

One of the most striking aspects of the first two Blair governments was the manner in which they made far-reaching alterations to the constitutional structure of the United Kingdom. More often than not those alterations were in many ways unsatisfactory, even unsustainable, and therefore contained within themselves the engines of further change. The House of Lords is a good example. There was a widespread view, by no means confined to the Left, that it was philosophically unacceptable that a small group of people had by inheritance a special influence in the government of the country. This state of affairs was clearly nonsensical. But although in the course of the twentieth century the powers of the Lords were further and further restricted, their privileged position nevertheless remained, however atrophied it had become.

Instead of recognising this as a glaring anomaly in the modern world, apologists didn't defend the system directly but argued instead that, while it had its shortcomings, anything that replaced it would inevitably be worse. If it were elected it would challenge the authority of the Commons; if it were nominated it would simply be full of 'Tony's Cronies'. It might not be perfect, pseudo-democrats insisted, but it worked. It was also the case, they asserted, that there lots of absolutely brilliant chaps in the Lords, leaders in their various fields, who would be lost to public service if an accident of birth hadn't put them into the legislature. The truth was that the vast majority of outstandingly talented people in the House of Lords had been placed there as life peers by various governments. The hereditaries were perhaps more typically represented by someone like the Earl of Clancarty who liked to explain to his fellow peers that he could trace his ancestry back to 63,000

BC, when beings from other planets landed on earth in space-ships. He also held the view, his *DailyTelegraph* obituary went on to explain in 1995, that: "A few of these early aliens did not come from space but emerged through tunnels from a civilisation which still existed beneath the earth's crust".

Well, something clearly had to be done, didn't it? But not much. A Labour government with a mighty majority hacked at the branches but not the tree itself. In 1999 most of the 750 hereditary peers had their voting rights abolished. But not all of them. Ninety-two remained in the Lords, elected by each other. In other words, the only eligible candidates for these places were the hereditary peers themselves, so in essence the old system remained. The question now is whether this new arrangement is so unsatisfactory, so manifestly absurd, that real reform will have to take place. To leave things as they are magnifies the original problem: it suggests that this was another of those matters of quantity and that what was wrong when applied to 750 people becomes all right when it involves only 92.

This is only one of the unresolved cases that demonstrate that attempts to introduce constitutional reforms tend not to settle old arguments but rather to start new ones. Nowhere more so than in Wales where only a few moments were allowed to pass between the establishment of the national assembly and the throat clearing of the massed voices of a chorus of complaint. Soon enough critics could ascribe every failure of policy and administration to the claim that the assembly wasn't 'a proper parliament'. Well, no, it wasn't. Nor was it meant to be. Indeed, that was what it was specifically meant *not* to be. Nor, come to that, was it possible for a dispassionate observer to grasp how 'a proper parliament' would solve problems like, say, the length of hospital waiting lists, which were surely a matter of managerial efficiency as much as anything. It was difficult to understand how, for instance, they might be legislated out of existence.

To wonder about such things is, as usual, to miss the point. A Welsh Assembly was created to meet the specific political needs of the Labour Party at a specific time, but in its turn that creation acquired its own political momentum, the gravitational pull that led it to seek greater influence and authority. In a short period of time such movements almost cease to be party political and become instead a test of institutional virility. What the members of the

assembly came to acquire was a shared interest in making themselves more influential in the broader scheme of things. Plaid
Cymru, by definition, wanted the institution to exercise more power
because the party had nothing more than a walk-on role in the rest
of Britain. It was an idea that also fitted snugly into the federalist
philosophy long propounded by the Liberal Democrats throughout
the UK. It was clear, too, that even the assembly Tories privately
totted up the advantages that might come to them. It's certainly the
case that, against all expectations, the Conservative Party was one
of the main beneficiaries of the devolution adventure.

Perhaps even more significant, though, is the special attraction
the assembly exerts on the imagination of some of its Labour
members, many of whom are old-fashioned people who continue
to look into the party's history for guidance on contemporary
conduct. Under this system a devolved administration can
distance itself (or say that it's doing so) from those policies of a
Labour government in Westminster of which it disapproves. In the
newspaper phrase, it can put something called 'clear red water'
between it and the fancy modernisers at the other end of the M4
motorway. Foundation hospitals? No fear. Not us. School tests and
league tables? Not on your life. We're *real* Labour down here.

One of the problems in the modern world, however, is that all
parties have an increasing difficulty in deciding what policies actually fit in with the traditions they are claiming to uphold. Down in
Cardiff Bay, for example, a Labour administration could present
itself as steadfastly loyal to some of the principles that had long
inspired the movement. This was an idea that informed an early
decision by the assembly government gradually to abolish
prescription charges in Wales. It looked like a specific piece of
homage to Aneurin Bevan, a studied reminder of his resignation
from the government in 1950 over the decision to introduce
charges on false teeth and spectacles supplied by the National
Health Service. Somehow, perhaps, the spirit of Bevan could be
restored at least in this Labour branch office.

It was a decision that was heavy on gesture but rather lighter
on practical advantage. When the scheme was introduced, something like 80 per cent of the prescriptions dispensed in Wales
weren't paid for anyway. Many classes of people were already
exempt for one reason or another. Those who still paid for their
prescriptions could afford to do so. The fundamental effect of the

measure would eventually be to take £30 million pounds from one area of health service spending and put it into the pockets of people who didn't actually need it. Those who cheered this policy as reflecting the spirit of old Labour were probably unaware that, as early as 1949, even Aneurin Bevan himself had had to concede, unwillingly, the principle of prescription charges.

In a small way, though, the point was being made that Wales could be different. It was made again in the summer of 2005. By this time the Labour government was in a minority in the assembly and found itself ambushed by a coalition of opposition parties who issued an ultimatum: increased university tuition fees, which were being introduced in England, should not apply in Wales. The idea was to avoid making it financially difficult for more young people, already threatened with large debts, to go to university. The official Conservative idea for achieving this was to cut the numbers going to university and so reduce opportunity in a wholly different way. Plaid Cymru and the Liberal Democrats simply wanted more public money to be made available for the purpose. This should have made for an uneasy alliance but, it became clear, it had little or nothing to do with political principle. This was a matter of exercising political power because it was possible to do so.

And it was a heady feeling. 'Hey, boys,' they said to one another. 'This is fun. Let's do it again.' Which they did. More tellingly, though, it provided further impetus in the quest for that thing called 'a proper parliament,' something that had nerves jangling in other areas of UK politics, not least among the Welsh Labour MPs.

That group could hear in the background the sound of stone on metal as a scythe was sharpened in preparation for cutting down at least some of their number. The essential cry from assembly expansionists, the definition of a 'proper' parliament, was for legislative powers. 'But,' MPs said to each other nervously in the Strangers' Bar, 'legislating is what *we* do. If that goes…' Goggle-eyed, they could hear the doors of the job centre creaking open.

An eventual reduction in their number was one of the implications of the findings of the Richard Commission which reported in March 2004 after almost two years of investigation into the powers of the assembly. It was chaired by Lord (Ivor) Richard, a Welshman, a QC, a former member of Tony Blair's Cabinet as Leader of the House of Lords, a former European Commissioner and, in the seventies, the British Ambassador to the United

Nations. It's difficult to think of anyone with more impressive credentials for the task. The nine commissioners represented the four main Welsh political parties and various areas of expertise including business and government administration. They held more than a hundred sessions to take evidence all over Wales and elsewhere. More than 300 people wrote to give their views. Their final report ran to more than 300 hundred pages. As you might expect with such a thorough, closely-argued, broad-based examination of the question, nothing more was heard about it.

Or not much. The truth was that it was all too rich for the Labour Party. It promised serious internal troubles because it would eventually mean cutting the number of Welsh MPs. Those MPs simply wouldn't wear it, even if the cut didn't take place, as was likely, for another ten years or so. Just as bad was the idea that the assembly should have eighty members rather than the present sixty, elected by Single Transferable Vote, a system that would pretty well guarantee that Labour could never hope to get anything that even looked like a majority. Ivor Richard was handing the party a rope and pointing out the location of the nearest tall tree.

There was outrage all round, naturally, or at least all round Plaid Cymru and the Liberal Democrats, at the idea that this long-awaited report was heading straight for the constitutional dustbin. But there was to be an unexpected sequel. A year or so later, against all expectations, the Labour Party itself came up with a scheme that was almost breathtaking in its ingenuity.

It proposed a number of changes in the relationship between the Welsh Assembly Government and the assembly itself, including a clear separation of powers which, it was agreed all round, was a necessary step forward. Less conventional, though, was the plan for an entirely new system which would extend the authority of the assembly as far as making laws was concerned, but which would still give the Westminster parliament a role in the process. More remarkable still was the proposal in the White Paper, *Better Governance for Wales*, that would create a mechanism whereby a referendum could eventually be triggered on the question of giving the assembly legislative powers over all devolved matters.

At this point in discussions of devolution over the years many ordinary men and women have found themselves growing heavy-lidded and wondering if there wasn't something on another channel. And who can blame them? In the journeys of political discovery the big questions for the uncommitted are always the identity of the destination, what they might find there, and the price of the ticket, rather than the names of every single station on the route. To put it in those terms, what was being proposed here was a single act of parliament under which, subject to various checks and balances, the assembly could gain substantial powers over large areas of Welsh life.

From a Labour point of view the attractions of this plan were that it postponed for some considerable time the business of addressing very touchy issues like how many Welsh MPs there should be and what sort of voting system should apply to the assembly itself. All such matters could be decided eventually, eventually being a very popular word in the political world since it carries the clear message that when the crucial time arrives those currently responsible will be long retired, or even dead. Better than that, these things didn't have to happen but they could if enough people wanted them. Even more gloriously from a government point of view was the fact that, while the details might be subject to all sorts of objections from more radical devolutionists, they were unlikely to carry their opposition to the point of wrecking the scheme. Some senior members of Plaid Cymru, for example, found themselves in a rare moment of agreement with each other when they privately described it as brilliant.* That reaction perhaps indicated a new, practical approach by Plaid Cymru, a party in which not absolutely everyone has an assured grip on political reality and its possibilities. But an even more revealing development has taken place where you might least have expected it: in the Conservative Party.

During the 2005 general election campaign the Tories argued that the devolution question in Wales should be settled by a new referendum. The voters would get the choice between leaving the assembly as it was, giving it more powers, or abolishing it. In these circumstances it was reasonable enough to ask the Conservative Leader, Michael Howard, how he would vote. Oh, he said, since he didn't live in Wales he wouldn't have a vote and therefore he couldn't say what he might do in what was necessarily a hypothetical set

---

* The flexibility and pragmatism of the scheme was illustrated by the fact that, at the back of the assembly's new debating chamber the architects placed a partition that could be easily removed to make room for an extra twenty members if numbers were ever increased.

of circumstances. This may well have been the first time in modern history that a leading politician has refused to express an opinion on his own party's policy,* but it was a revealing move nonetheless.

The truth was that although the Conservatives had been unswerving opponents of devolution in general and, above all, of Welsh devolution, actual experience of it had made them think again, although they didn't say so in such terms. The very existence of an assembly had saved their bacon when it came to the question of there being any kind of credible Conservative presence in Wales. They didn't win a single Welsh parliamentary seat in 1997 or in 2001. They managed to get one of the 40 first past the post seats in the assembly in 1999. But the fact that a system of proportional representation gave them another eight members meant access to those essential signifiers of continuing political life, coverage in the newspapers and on television and radio.

Better than that, devolution also created a new class of professional politicians who could use their assembly seats to achieve other ambitions. So in 2005, David Davies (the only Tory first past the post-er) became MP for Monmouth as well as its assembly representative. David Jones, who had served a brief period in the assembly, won Clwyd West. Jonathan Morgan, who had been a full-time politician since the age of 24, came close to defeating Labour in Cardiff North. In the 2003 elections the party was on the brink of becoming the official opposition in the assembly, with 11 seats to Plaid Cymru's 12. This was why what had once been the unflinching party of unionism began to see, in Wales at least, the advantages of becoming the rather more flexible party of devolution. After all, when Labour politicians in the eighties despaired of ever again exercising power at Westminster, they began to look at what they might achieve in alternative centres of influence like the institutions of the EU, or through the future establishment of devolved parliaments in the UK. In their turn the Tories learnt the lesson.

In these circumstances Michael Howard was clearly right to say nothing, not least because of the fact that any proposal to take away the Welsh Assembly, however inadequate and unpopular it

* Early in 2006 Michael Howard was easily outdone in this respect by Rhodri Morgan who refused to say whether he was for or against the Iraq war. He claimed that since he had ceased to be an MP at the time of the crucial vote it wasn't something on which he needed to express a point of view. When asked how he might have voted he said: "I don't know, I have not looked at the issues. I am not in the House of Commons."

was, would almost certainly have exposed him to sustained accusations of being anti-democratic. That probability is borne out by the fact that when, shortly afterwards, he tried to reduce the democratic element in the organisation of his own party's leadership contests he was sharply rebuffed by its members.

This brief excursion into the undergrowth of constitutional policy leaves out many of the details, but one thing emerges with great clarity. Although it was always difficult to detect any logical pattern in the Blair government's approach to devolution, in the end it stumbled on what by their standards was a more or less coherent position. The prospect was that in the foreseeable future Northern Ireland (people assumed, with fingers crossed) Scotland and Wales were all likely to have institutions that gave them a substantial measure of self-government. They wouldn't be exactly the same in all cases, but roughly equivalent. Once again, though, it was impossible to regard this as the point at which this progress would suddenly be arrested. New and tantalising questions would remain unanswered.

Not the least of those was the matter of England. It became clear towards the end of 2004 that there was little appetite for setting up regional assemblies that would match those in the three nations. By a majority of well over three to one, voters in the North East turned down such a scheme, something that prompted the cancellation of referendums in other areas. So the question persisted: how was England itself to be governed? More accurately, perhaps, how was England to govern itself?

This had always been perhaps the most inconvenient of the issues that was raised by the question of devolution. It had been propounded most forcibly in the seventies by the Scottish Labour MP, Tam Dalyell, in the form of the West Lothian Question, so called after the name of his then constituency: how was it possible to justify Members of Parliament from Scotland and Wales voting on matters that affected England only, while English MPs would not be able to vote on the same issues as they affected Scotland and Wales? The Welsh aspect of this was readily answered. Since a Welsh Assembly would have no legislative powers the matter didn't arise. In Scotland, though, it was different, and the answer was an uneasy compromise: cut the number of Scottish MPs. After all, this had for many years been the answer to a similar question asked about Northern Ireland when it was governed from Stormont. The

province had only 12 MPs at Westminster, fewer than its population would have justified, until the number was raised to 17 in
1983, after the imposition of direct rule. In the same way one of the
consequences of establishing a Scottish Parliament was the reduction, from 2005, in the number of Scotland's MPs from 72 to 59.

The continuing problem is that a simple reduction in the
number of MPs doesn't address the central question which is this:
why are *any* of these people voting at all on matters that don't
affect the lives of the people they represent. Why, for example,
should the votes of Scottish members be decisive in the matter of
fees charged by English universities? It's a puzzle that exercises
Conservative minds more than most since the party has managed
to win only two Scottish seats in three general elections from 1997
onwards. At the same time the Tories in Wales went two elections
without getting a single seat before winning three in 2005. No
wonder leading figures in the Tory Party think there's something
in this issue that might ring bells with the voters of middle
England. At least two of the contenders for the party leadership at
the end of 2005 talked of this as being 'unfinished business'. A
little while later William Hague, resuming a prominent role on the
Opposition front bench, raised the matter again.

But there is even more compelling evidence that this is a problem of real substance. It lies in the insistence of Labour ministers
that it isn't. One of them told me that the government didn't want
to see British politics 'balkanised', while the Lord Chancellor,
Lord Falconer, had to dig into the nat-bashing rhetoric of the
seventies to make the same point. In March 2006 he argued that
an English parliament would lead to the break-up of the United
Kingdom. "Devolution is not a stepping stone to a federal state,"
he said. "That would be an open goal to the nationalists."

As long as they continue to have substantial majorities Labour
governments will thumb their noses when reminded of this anomaly, but one day there will be a UK government that isn't Labour
and the boot will go in. The consequence could well be that, for
certain specific purposes, the Westminster parliament will turn
itself into an England-only body. At the same time, of course, we
can feel certain that there won't be Conservative administrations
in Scotland and Wales (and definitely not in Northern Ireland
because the Conservative Party doesn't contest seats there, any
more than do Labour and the Liberal Democrats). In other words,

many more opportunities will be created for disputes between the
national parliaments and the authority of Westminster.

In these circumstances, which are bound to arise, given the
cyclical nature of UK politics, the power Aneurin Bevan sought so
diligently through the various institutions of government in Britain
might set out on its travels once more. The decline of philosophical passion which at Westminster has erased so many arguments
over principle, may persuade energetic political activists that they
can have a more influential role closer to their own communities.
However, this is not something that would necessarily be confined
to the UK's devolved administrations. Conservatives above all are
being urged to adopt the idea of 'localism', otherwise known as
'soft government', as a way of reviving their party's fortunes.
Admittedly it's not an idea that is currently on everyone's lips. Its
chief cheerleader is the newspaper columnist and former *Times*
editor, Simon Jenkins, who thinks it lies at the heart of what he
believes is now the greatest ideological divide in modern Britain:
between those who believe in a centralised bureaucracy and those
who support local autonomy. Adopting the latter, its supporters
believe, would be a way of revitalising democracy, reawakening
people's interest in the way in which they are governed, inspired
by the ability to make serious decisions close to home about levels
of taxation and the ways in which the money is spent.

It would be unwise to put more than a few Euros on the
prospect of this idea setting fire to the public imagination. The
dismal record of local government in places like Wales, most
famously the endemic corruption that was for a long time its
notable characteristic in many areas, would make any sensible
voter wary about trusting local councillors or their modern equiv-
alents with much more power than they exercise at present. But at
the same time there's no denying that there's a trend in this direction, fuelled by the development of devolved institutions. Above all
it's an indication of the way in which a ill-defined scheme for
moving a few bricks from one part of the wall to another can alter
the entire nature of the structure. What governments intend to
happen is often confounded by the eventual, and often unfore-
seen, consequences of their policies

OLD MEN IN A HURRY

THE WHOLE BUSINESS of Scottish and Welsh devolution began as the preferred answer to a pressing political question: how could Labour dish the nats? That's putting it crudely, perhaps, but that's how politicians often talk in private, as Downing Street memoirs have revealed in recent years. In his book *Final Term*, by no means the most interesting political memoir ever written, Harold Wilson was rather more delicate about the matter. Despite the fact that the narrative covered the years 1974 to 1976, the period when the whole devolution issue came to the centre of British political life, he didn't actually find it necessary to make any mention at all of Plaid Cymru. As for the Scottish National Party, they got only a brief look-in in Wilson's account of his speech to parliament on the 1975 devolution White Paper.

"The first aim," he wrote, "was as far as possible to put the Scottish National Party in baulk by giving the Scots a clear choice between a greater control over their own affairs, nearer their home, through the Scottish Assembly, and ministers responsible to it, as against SNP separatism".

Well, that's clear enough. Devolution was a political strategy rather than some kind of principled measure aimed at improving the government of the United Kingdom. But then, who but a few obsessives thought it was anything else, even though elsewhere Wilson dressed it up in a more statesmanlike but strangely unenticing manner. "Devolution," he wrote, "is a boring word, a boring and soporific subject as far as legislation is concerned, but potentially a most powerful means of achieving one of the highest aims of democracy, bringing the process of decision-making as close as possible to the people affected by it."

It's interesting to note how quick-witted politicians often discover that a strategy that's just the thing they need in order to resolve some passing crisis also turns out to be a visionary policy that will improve the condition of the general population in matchless ways. It's not unlike the poses struck by those who, dumped by the Labour Party, set up in opposition and announce that, actually, they were socialists all along. Still, the point about politics is winning and, thirty years after Wilson, it's possible to argue that, in an entirely unexpected way, the strategy worked in the short term. If not totally dished, the nats, who between them won fourteen seats in Scotland and Wales in the autumn election of 1974, certainly went into something of a decline. In 1974, for example, the SNP had eleven MPs. The best they've done since then is six, in 1997 and again in 2005. When you recall the dramas of that period, a time when the failure of the devolution plans was the immediate occasion for the 1979 election, this is strikingly curious.

In that election the SNP, which had held 11 seats, had its representation reduced to two, hardly the symptom of a country in a ferment of desire for self-determination and furious at having it snatched away. Plaid Cymru, which had less clout and less support, jogged along with a couple of seats or so and a popular vote lurking around the ten per cent mark. You could have been forgiven for thinking that five long years of the devolution topic had been quite enough for a large section of the general public.

And then the question arises, why did it make such a spectacular comeback? And why did it do so under Tony Blair, a man who had never been known to express any interest in the subject, never mind enthusiasm for it? Why do something that might prod those slumbering nats into a refreshed consciousness? The answer lay with Blair's predecessor, John Smith, a man whose influence on his party continued from beyond the grave. During the interminable attempts to legislate on devolution during the seventies, Michael Foot, as Lord President of the Council in the Callaghan government, was the man in charge of getting it onto the statute book. He was an enthusiast, as was Smith, the talented and sociable Scottish lawyer who was his deputy, and whose able performance in the role secured him promotion to the Cabinet in the twilight days of that administration. When he succeeded Neil Kinnock as Labour leader in 1992, Smith wrote devolution firmly back into the programme of a future Labour government.

Blair might well have been inclined to drop it but, according to his biographer, Anthony Seldon, he was strong-armed by the very powerful Scottish mafia in the Shadow Cabinet, a group that included

Gordon Brown, Robin Cook, Donald Dewar and George Robertson.
Seldon writes: "They made it clear they would never allow it to
be dropped and the Liberal Democrats, whom Blair was courting,
were also very keen, so he agreed... to let it go ahead." Seldon goes
on to say that Blair's only important contribution to the scheme
was to insist that referendums should be included in the party's
draft manifesto. It was an unpopular move with some of the pro-
devolutionists. Rhodri Morgan, then the MP for Cardiff West, was
described as shaking with rage, presumably because he, as well as
many of the Scottish MPs, thought that referendums would once
again wreck the whole scheme, as they had in 1979. This time,
though, they had the opposite effect. Because the referendums
were held quickly, and before rather than after legislation, they
pre-empted any serious obstruction in parliament. They could be
waved around as a democratic mandate, after all, however tattered
the result might have looked in Wales.
Seldon says that Blair was particularly unenthusiastic about
Welsh devolution. Maybe a couple of years later he thought his
instincts were right over this, as they had been over the referendums.
When the results started coming in from the first assembly elections, Downing Street began to echo to cries of "fucking Welsh," as
the Prime Minister realised Labour wouldn't get a majority. That at
least is the version noted by a former senior spin doctor, Lance
Price, in the diaries he kept during his time working for Blair.*
However, there appears to have been no indication that Blair paused
for a moment to consider whether he himself might have had some
responsibility for this state of affairs, arising from his determination
that Alun Michael should lead Labour in Wales and the old-fashioned fixing by party apparatchiks necessary to accomplish that
aim. But then, in politics someone else is pretty well always to blame,
as Price makes clear. What emerged, he recorded, was "a widespread view that devolution had been a terrible idea. Everyone
claimed to have believed all along that it would lead to disaster."
Blair's intervention on behalf of Alun Michael was unpopular
and damaging, but in normal circumstances even a flagrant disregard for anyone else's point of view needn't have been much of a

---

* It being Britain, the most senior civil servant in the land, the Cabinet Secretary,
insisted that this remark was cut from the published version of the diaries. It being
Wales, someone reported Blair to the North Wales Police. It being the North Wales

problem. However, these were not normal circumstances. The rules had been rewritten. A system of proportional representation meant that Labour, perhaps in a moment of post-election, triumphalist inattention, had broken one of the most sacred rules in its Masonic handbook: it had handed power to someone else. Without proportional representation, devolution would have been a one-party farce; with it, it was unpredictable and almost exciting.

The immediate consequences of minority government in Wales are well known. The assembly's sacking of Alun Michael and his replacement by Rhodri Morgan; an eventual coalition between Labour and the Liberal Democrats; an election in which Labour got exactly half the seats; some more banana skins, which we'll come to, and so back to minority government. In these circumstances the chief beneficiary simply had to be the main opposition group, those nats again. This was the point at which Plaid Cymru would surely establish itself as a potential party of government. It had intercepted the other side's pass and the line was at its mercy. Then it showed the world just how deeply the party was steeped in Welsh tradition: it dropped the ball.

In some ways the story of how Plaid Cymru stumbled on the very brink of an unprecedented opportunity isn't really about Wales at all. It's about politics as practised in many parts of the world, particularly in Britain. Above all it's about the kind of people who are driven by political ambition and the crucial nature of their relationships with each other. Gordon v Tony has been the long-running drama playing at Westminster, but Welsh theatre has its own version, with a different cast, now in its umpteenth record-breaking year.

In fact it's striking how political parties tend to ape each other's fashions, using the same language, employing similar techniques, even mimicking each other's gestures. In the summer of 1995, for example, the then Prime Minister, John Major, announced that he had decided to stand down as leader of the Conservative Party. At the same time, he explained, he would also be a candidate in the election consequently needed to fill the vacancy he had thus created. The farcical nature of this event, and its failure to bring Major any discernible benefit, proved to be in no way a deterrent when, a few years later, another leader suddenly announced to a baffled public that he too would be resigning but, it turned out later, only up to a point.

This time the resignation was from not one but two posts at the head of his party. He would stay in office until the jobs had been filled, he said, but after that he'd be on his way. When the time came to elect his replacements, however, he said that he'd decided after all that he would be standing for a position which, at that time, he already held. In the event he won, although only by an authority-sapping handful of votes, and resumed office with the comment that this sort of contest was good for his party.

These procedures took place in the period from May to September 2003 and the politician in question was Ieuan Wyn Jones, who was both President of Plaid Cymru and the party's leader in the National Assembly. When the process finished he was no longer president but still in charge in the assembly. Thus his main achievement was to increase by one the substantial crowd of elected leaders of one kind or another who jostled with one another at the top end of the Plaid Cymru organisation. It was difficult to see how this improved anything at all and, indeed, how it could fail to damage further such esteem as Ieuan Wyn Jones enjoyed inside and outside his party.

The chief obstacle in writing about politics is not that information is difficult to come by, but that too much is pressed upon you. Just as witnesses to traffic accidents often disagree over the details, so the participants in a political pile-up recollect what happened in a slightly different way. More often than not it's not a case of people telling lies (although sometimes it is) but rather a combination of imperfections of memory added to a perfectly natural desire to be seen as both honourable and wise. So in the case of Ieuan Wyn Jones and the reasons for his resignation and his resurrection, it's perhaps as well to steer clear of the reported details of who did what to whom and instead attempt briefly to construct a plausible version of the story.

In the days after the 2003 assembly elections Ieuan Wyn Jones's dilemma stemmed from the understandable disappointment felt within the party about its performance. Before the vote it had held seventeen seats; that number had fallen to twelve. That was made all the worse by all the optimistic pre-election talk of great gains sweeping Plaid Cymru perhaps even as far as that mountain ridge from which they might glimpse a prospect of eventually winning a majority. Ieuan Wyn was blamed for this failure, not least for the very good reason that he was party leader, and therefore paid to take the blame. When things go wrong party leaders are by definition at fault, but he was slightly more suspect than usual because of the loss of his Westminster seat, Ynys Môn, to Labour when he stood down at the previous general election. It was a powerful and specific indication, critics felt, of his shortcomings as a political strategist.

Whether this dissatisfaction led to a plot to get rid of him is problematical, but it seems most likely that what began as generalised grumbling among some assembly members led quickly to a position where, if not actively campaigning to sack him, they were quite happy to give him a push through the exit. A message via the chair of the assembly group, Dr Dai Lloyd, that six of the twelve members wanted to see 'some change' in the leadership was interpreted by Ieuan Wyn as a vote of no confidence. He replied by saying that his position was untenable and that he would therefore resign.

In the claustrophobic world of Welsh politics this was seen as something of a sensation at the time, but it's now clear that it was really a sideshow, consisting essentially of a tentative move against Ieuan Wyn which provoked an impetuous response from the man himself. Perhaps, fed up and feeling unloved, he really meant to go. If he meant to stay it was, as petulant resignations usually are, a dangerous strategy. If one of his assembly colleagues had been elected president, rather than the veteran folk singer/demagogue Dafydd Iwan, he would have lost all leadership roles. As it was he only survived as party leader in the assembly with a majority of 71 out of more than 5,000 votes. Half a busload of people voting the other way would have seen him off. Not only that, but in the first ballot he had come second to his main rival, Helen Mary Jones, the rumbustious and impulsive figure who was widely suspected of being the moving spirit behind a plan to get rid of him. She denied it, but at the same time she didn't make any secret of her lack of enthusiasm for his abilities as a leader. What had happened, in summary, was that when Ieuan Wyn asked who should take on the job he already had, almost exactly half his party said it should be someone other than him. The surprising thing is that it didn't prove fatal, as it had done in Mrs Thatcher's case in 1990.

Again, as with John Major, this might have been classified as a pretty daft way of going on. Both men were making forlorn attempts to assert their authority over divided parties, perhaps hoping by a show of brinkmanship to silence at least some of the ceaseless dissent of their critics, maybe even believing that resignation, like a bucket of cold water in a dogfight, would bring an end at least to some of the yapping and bickering. Such a desperate measure was an indication of how serious they believed their plight to be. But it was never going to effective because both men were confronted with a much deeper problem, one about which they could do nothing. John Major's chief difficulty was that he wasn't Margaret Thatcher, Ieuan Wyn Jones's that he wasn't Dafydd Wigley. Worse than that, both men were seen by opponents within their parties as inadequate replacements for great leaders who had been toppled by the illegitimate methods of lesser people.

Another fashion in modern politics has been to alter the language used to describe internal party disputes. Opposing groups are no longer described as left and right, but instead are characterised as modernisers against traditionalists. To some extent this is a useful way of translating the rivalries, often as much personal as philosophical, that have always existed in all political organisations. Far from being an exception to this rule, for many years Plaid Cymru came to exemplify it.

In its case it could be reduced to a simple fixture list: Dafydd v Dafydd, that's to say Dafydd Wigley, captain of the traditionalists, against Dafydd Elis-Thomas, leading the modernisers. The idea is that Wigley has been in some sense the keeper of the cultural traditions of Welsh nationalism, putting the Welsh language and its welfare close to the top of the political agenda. The other Dafydd, always known as Dafydd El, fiercely rejects the label of nationalist and believes that campaigns on behalf of the language and what stems from them are not the proper concern of serious politicians. It's a useful enough distinction between the two men, although it's pretty thin in many places, but, curiously, a brief reading of their backgrounds and careers would lead the unwary to suspect that their views would be the other way around.

Wigley is unmistakably middle class, the son of a senior local government official in north Wales, educated at a public school and Manchester University, a physicist by training who worked as a cost accountant, the least romantic of professions, for a number of multinational companies. Dafydd El is a son of the manse, middle class in its way, too, but certainly not in the material sense. An intellectual and academic, he is steeped in the works of the great figures of Welsh literature, a field about which he was enthusiastic enough to complete his doctorate while serving as a Member of Parliament.

In style Wigley might at any time have been mistaken for a dili-
gent and capable practitioner in the mainstream of British politics.
It's not hard to visualise him as a Labour minister, for example. It's
not that he lacks a Welsh identity, it's just not the first or second
thing that strikes you about him. For that reason he's sometimes
made a point, as he's said himself, of emphasising his Welsh
language credentials (making a speech in Welsh where using
English might get him better publicity, for example) in a way that
reassures those who might think that someone of his background
was in some way suspect: that he was not totally, truly, viscerally
Welsh in the manner demanded by the small but noisy group of
self-appointed thought police on the outer fringes of nationalism.
To other audiences he sometimes makes political capital out of the
fact that he was born in Derby.

For his part, Dafydd El, who claims to dream in English, sees
no need to wave his Welsh identity card at every checkpoint. If
challenged, indeed, he'd be more likely to tear it up as a gesture of
defiance. He is deeply and publicly contemptuous of many of the
cherished attitudes of the cultural campaigners. One of their
famous victories was the establishment of a Welsh language television channel, S4C, achieved because of a threat by the then Plaid
Cymru president, Gwynfor Evans, to starve himself to death if the
government, under Mrs Thatcher, did not keep its promise to
establish such a service. Dafydd El insists that such narrow aims
and grandstanding of this nature have no place in real politics.

A decision to flood a Welsh valley and drown the village of Capel
Celyn in order to create a reservoir to supply the needs of the people
of Liverpool was one of the key conflicts of the sixties that politicised
people like Wigley, then a schoolboy. It was a gift to Welsh nationalism, which has always been crowded with prospectors panning for
nuggets of English oppression; Dafydd El snorts with impatience at
the suggestion that a political party can be constructed on a series of
complaints and resentments rather than substantial ideas of political
progress and the structures that go with them. Its not that the causes
are inherently unworthy, simply that they are a distraction. He is
caustically unsympathetic to the refrain in some strands of nationalist politics that the Welsh have been in some way the victims of the
English down the ages and continue to be so. The idea that most of
the problems of Wales stem from gleeful English malevolence is
something he seems to regard as juvenile folly.

If I understand him correctly, his view is that Welsh politics should be no different from any other politics: it should be about attaining power and using that to create a desirable social and political order. Cultural considerations would be part of that, as they are in any society, but they would not be the objectives by which other achievements were judged. In the meantime pressure groups should get on with whatever it is pressure groups do, while a political party like Plaid Cymru should create or embrace the institutions that are essential to the existence of a nation. His unvarnished way of putting these arguments, above all his dismissive attitude to something like the Gwynfor Evans' fast, heroic to many nationalists, irrelevant to him, may owe more than a little to his taste for controversy. Sometimes you can't avoid the impression that he sees tact as an overrated component in political strategy.

Saying all this, it's tempting to assess the gap between him and Wigley as being the traditional one between left and right. In one sense that is – or at least was – true. If you had to make a stab at placing Wigley on the British political spectrum it would be somewhere on the (not very far) left of the Labour Party, but certainly identifiable as a believer in the intervention of government to promote social and economic equality. Socialist, in a moderate, old-fashioned way, is a word he'd probably be comfortable with, but, as Laura McAllister records in her book on Plaid Cymru, his own chosen label is that of pragmatic radical. His aim is to make politics work rather than forcing it conform to some theory or other.

Dafydd El's views are more difficult to pin down and have become more so as the years have gone on. Marxist to begin with certainly, far left in what was not always a well-defined way, inclined to talk in terms of the need to "mobilise the Welsh working class", internationalist, notably in his enthusiasm to make Plaid Cymru a European party, keen on causes like CND and the various manifestations of the gender and sexual politics of the late twentieth century. As the Marxist left has become marginalised, so it's grown increasingly difficult to detect in him a consistent line, but within him too, there is surely more than an element of pragmatism.

Wigley and Dafydd El are both men of very strong passions. In Wigley's case you sometimes think that he cares so much about some cause that he will surely explode in a starburst of fury and frustration. *Sotto voce* is a concept with which he is entirely unfamiliar; he booms away as if every conversation were some form of public meeting. He relishes political combat and when angry makes no allowances, so that entirely innocent people might find themselves denounced at second hand for a transgression for which someone else – or no one at all – is to blame. There is a perpetual sense of intensity about him, a permanent impression of being late for something, not least because, like most dedicated politicians, he crams his day with duties of one kind or another. Like all dedicated politicians, too, he makes no bones about wanting his own way, a trait that in the end always leads to some kind of trouble.

Dafydd El wants his own way too, but he tends to glide where Wigley barges. He is one of those people you find in politics who, even when they are in fact wondering whether to have their eggs poached or scrambled, give off an air of calculation and guile. He can get angry too. When the Plaid Cymru Assembly Members provoked Ieuan Wyn Jones's resignation, he went to the members' tea room and denounced them to their faces. Their action, he thought, indicated a lack of loyalty and of party discipline. Yet in the same breath as he discusses this matter he can also say, unblushingly, that, because he is the assembly's Presiding Officer, a kind of Speaker, he plays no part in the internal affairs of his party. In such ways he's notably adaptable, and just as capable in other circumstances of uttering soothing words and encouragement rather than a rebuke. You only have to look at a career in which, time and again, he has floated to the surface clutching some prize or other, to recognise that he has a highly-developed understanding of the mechanics of public and political life.

Neither man owes much to the grim social traditions of Welsh Nonconformity. While it would be wrong to describe Wigley as sybaritic, he has a keen appreciation of good living, although from his conventional appearance you might think he was still practising his trade of cost accountancy. For his part, Dafydd El pays serious attention to the quality of things like food and drink. He is fastidious about his appearance. When a former girlfriend gave a revenge interview to a glossy magazine she claimed that, even in times of severe financial pressure, he would still buy designer clothes, although sometimes they had to be hidden under the bed. His comment was that, yes, he did buy designer clothes, but only in the sales.

This matter of appearance, the studied care he takes, go further than just modish personal taste. In his years as the assembly's Presiding Officer he has emerged as being rather more than a little presidential. On the weekend you might come across him in something green and tweedy, as though he was just back from shooting a bit of wildlife. Or perhaps he'll be sporting a pair of startlingly yellow corduroy trousers or, in summer, a rakishly-worn straw hat; or again he might be in the sober outfit suitable for Sunday morning service at Llandaff Cathedral, where he is a regular attender. This is all the more fun, and maybe he finds it so, because of the fact that such display drives the many class warriors who remain in Plaid Cymru mad with disapproval. They see it as a deadly combination of affectation and betrayal. And they hate it all the more because he is, as Lord Elis-Thomas of Nant Conwy in the County of Gwynedd, a member of the House of Lords. Worse than that, he clearly enjoys being so.

These two contrasting figures, Dafydd Wigley and Dafydd Elis-Thomas, are among the most interesting, engaging and accomplished politicians in modern Wales. You don't have to agree with them to appreciate the contribution they have made to the development of the idea of Wales as a place where people might take more of the decisions about their lives. But there's also no escaping the fact that their rivalry, which has run for decades, has been a key influence on the fortunes of their party. In the tensions between them and their consequences, their story anticipates that of Gordon and Tony. And, like the Labour men, they began as allies in the process of reinventing and invigorating their party. More than thirty years later they may bring their careers to a close by reviving just that relationship.

As we've seen in so many political lives, chance played an important part in their progress. A mortal illness, three votes in a single constituency and Ted Heath's miscalculation were among the factors that unexpectedly opened the doors into long political careers. Who would have forecast it, even as late as the mid-sixties when there seemed to be little room in Wales for anything that looked like political pluralism. In the 1966 general election Labour won thirty-two of the thirty-six seats, the Conservatives three and the Liberals one. But to think that Wales had become uniformly Labour or even that Labour meant the same thing all over the country would have been a mistake.

In rural Wales, for example, party labels were rather less important than the character and reputation of the individual candidates. So many of those who after the war became Labour

MPs in the north and west were exactly the same type of people who would previously have been Liberals. Their views wouldn't have been all that different, either. Cledwyn Hughes (later Lord Cledwyn of Penrhos) who won Anglesey for Labour in 1951 and who was to become a Cabinet Minister, was a good example of that. An even more spectacular example of the indifference voters could display towards nominal party allegiances was provided by Elystan Morgan (now Lord Elystan-Morgan) who in 1964 was the Plaid Cymru candidate for Merioneth, where he came third. Fewer than eighteen months later he was winning Cardigan for Labour, snatching the seat from the incumbent Liberal.

In the same way it seems likely that in 1974 the two Dafydds benefited from an inclination for a tiny element of novelty among the voters of Caernarfon and Merioneth. So the constituencies switched from their Labour members, of whom perhaps they were growing a little weary, and happily voted in a couple of guys from Plaid Cymru, seeing them as the sort of bright young people who could maintain the general political traditions of their essentially conservative areas. In this regard Dafydd Elis Thomas's avowed Marxism seems to have caused very little by way of comment or concern.

Two other factors helped. In the two Plaid Cymru victories, as in many other matters, Heath's decision to call a 'who rules Britain?' election was pivotal. Not the Conservatives, the voters grumbled, but maybe not Labour either. They delivered an answer steeped in doubt. There was no overall majority for anyone, and parties around the fringe received some modest benefits. The number of Liberal seats went up from six to fourteen, the Scottish National Party from one to seven and, for the first time at a general election, Plaid Cymru got into Westminster.

It's possible, though, that the two seats concerned would never have been won for the party in the first place if it hadn't been for a spectacular by-election victory by Gwynfor Evans in Carmarthen in 1966. The fact that, against all expectations, Plaid had finally got a parliamentary seat was something that tore down a psychological barrier and altered attitudes among voters and campaigners alike. But then, that by-election wouldn't have taken place at all if the Labour member, Lady Megan Lloyd George, encouraged by Harold Wilson, hadn't continued as a candidate despite the fact that she was mortally ill. Six weeks after the general election she was dead and Gwynfor got his unique opportunity.

Even that, though, wasn't the end of the intervention of chance in these affairs. Gwynfor lost Carmarthen in 1970 and in the first election of 1974 failed by three votes to win it back from Labour. So it was that the two Dafydds spent their first months at Westminster free of the presence of their leader, a man of an authoritarian cast of mind and unyielding seriousness of purpose, a sixty-one-year-old teetotaller whose idea of a good day out did not include the cross-party bonhomie that suffuses much of Westminster life. The two young men (31 and 28) had six months to immerse themselves in a metropolitan whirl made all the more fascinating by the parliamentary arithmetic. Every vote, theirs as much as anyone's, could be decisive on several days of any week. By the time Gwynfor won Carmarthen again, in October of that year, they were well established in the conventions of the Palace of Westminster and temperamentally beyond recall to less congenial traditions.

The eyes of many people in the British political world, practitioners and commentators, brim with nostalgic tears when they look back to that period. In those years from 1974 to 1979 Parliament really counted and persistent uncertainty made nervous wrecks of those charged with keeping the machinery of government running. On many, many nights, until the government and opposition tellers walked together down the centre of the chamber after a vote, you couldn't be certain who was going to win on any issue. Business often went on into the early hours of the morning while MPs snatched what sleep they could in their office armchairs. If there was a vote even more vital than usual, ambulances containing seriously ill members would be driven into New Palace Yard. A Whip would check that they were actually still alive before they were 'nodded through', that's to say had their votes counted without their having to go through the lobbies, a process that might have killed some of them. Perhaps some of this was barely civilised, but there's no denying that it was often exciting.

For much of this period, too, Wales and Scotland were at the centre of the tumult as the government pressed on with its devolution plans, assailed with as much vigour from its own side as from the official opposition. This was the wheeze that was designed to deliver those nationalist votes for as long as the legislation struggled its way through parliament. So those three Plaid Cymru members had an influence out of all proportion to their numbers as they were wooed and pampered and had their temperatures taken by the various ministerial nursemaids assigned to see to their welfare.

In these circumstances the impressive range of political philosophies they spanned between them wasn't a matter of pressing concern. Gywnfor, the stubborn, romantic nationalist, Wigley, the leftish pragmatist, and Dafydd El, the Marxist with a million causes, had one unifying objective: to do whatever was necessary to get a scheme for Welsh devolution onto the statute book. When, in 1979, it all turned to ashes, visits from senior figures in other parties ceased abruptly. They were now free to pursue their own ideological rainbows.

Gwynfor was the freest of them since he lost his seat in the 1979 election, in what turned out to be a prelude to what, in the context of his long and unswerving career, his greatest individual achievement. It was his last campaign. Only he could have done it; he was probably the only man in the world who would have been believed when he said he would kill himself over a television service.

When it was over he finally retired as the party's president, at the age of almost seventy and after thirty-six years in office. The contest for the succession was, inevitably, between the two Dafydds. Many people saw it as another of those choices between left and right, the source of enduring factionalism in all parties. Nor was it an unfair way of putting it since Dafydd El was unmistakeably to the left of Wigley and, indeed, to the left of the majority of people in mainstream British politics. This is perhaps where all the trouble began.

*

The details of the divisions between Wigley and Dafydd El, the growing estrangement that was to mark their relationship over the coming decades, are difficult to pin down precisely. Nor do they matter very much in the broader scheme of things. That they existed at all was the important point. In essence, as I say, they are Blair and Brown under different banners, each seeking authority over the style and substance of their party. These things get very personal.

When Wigley became president of Plaid Cymru in 1981, the party was still reeling from the devolution referendum held two years previously. The Welsh public had contemptuously rejected the scheme by a majority of four to one. Not a single county could

muster a majority for it. What on earth could a party of self-government do to seduce voters who thought that even a modest advance
in that direction was a charade? Well, of course, it could always get
out the old political umbrella and seek shelter under the idea that
people had rejected that proposal because they could see how inadequate it was, that it didn't go far enough. There were a few people
who could say such things without laughing, but the danger clearly
was that the party, having seen its modest prize snatched away,
might have fragmented into the factionalism and impossibilism that
overwhelmed Labour at exactly that time. That path might have
been all the more tempting as the theme of much political activism
became what was portrayed as the monstrous nature of the
Thatcher government and its apparent invulnerability to the usual
methods of opposition; even to those methods outside the normal
democratic tradition that were to be tested to destruction by the
miners' strike. In Wales many people who wouldn't recognise
colliery winding gear if it fell on their heads felt there was something
personal in that last battle for the coal industry.

The tribute people understandably pay to Wigley is that such
things didn't happen under his presidency. His attitude towards
rebuilding the party perhaps owed something to the fact that he
was no longer some obscure Welsh politician trying to shove his
foot in the establishment's front door. As happens with many
people, Westminster had changed him in terms of authority and
expertise, not least because he (and Dafydd El) wasn't suffocated
by inhabiting a purely Welsh political world.

But the progress of Plaid Cymru's revival as led by Wigley was to
be interrupted by the most melancholy circumstances. On that day
in 1974 when Edward Heath had called a general election, Wigley
and his wife, the harpist Elinor Bennett, had been told that their sons
Alun, then aged two, and Geraint, one, had a congenital illness that
meant they would not survive into adulthood. Wigley had continued
with his political career, but by 1984 his sons' health had markedly
declined (two later children, another son and a daughter, were not
affected by the condition) and he resigned from the presidency. The
two boys died within weeks of each other the following year. It was
an experience that inspired Wigley to become a campaigner on
matters connected with disability, something he carried out with his
habitual passion, on one occasion breaking the arm on the Speaker's
chair as MPs voted on a bill dealing with embryo research.

Dafydd Wigley's approach as president was always wrapped up in his central aim of making Plaid Cymru a party that would be an alternative to, and eventually a replacement for, Labour, above all in industrial South Wales. This is, after all, the place where the vast majority of Welsh voters live, a psephological fact of life sometimes lost on those who are preoccupied with the cultural aspects of policy. Wales is a country divided in so many ways – north and south, east and west, urban and rural, Welsh-speaking and monoglot English – that the natural condition of those who live in one part is suspicion and ignorance of those who live in the others. Anyone who aspires to lead Plaid Cymru successfully has to persuade them all that their individual interests can be reconciled, particularly those relating to the Welsh language.

Or perhaps there's another way, which is to relegate those specific concerns to the political second division of pressure group agitation and instead persuade the general population that they can build a broader and consensus in the interests of everyone involved. That's one way of describing the approach taken by Dafydd Elis Thomas when he succeeded Dafydd Wigley as president in 1984. His vision of Plaid Cymru was of a party that looked outward, espcially in a European context, and which played a part in advancing supra-national movements like nuclear disarmament and environmental conservation. It was an attempt to fit Wales into an entirely new political dispensation that shoved the usual nation state preoccupations into a back seat. Dafydd El's personal commitment to such ideals was embodied in his decision, in 1989, to run for the European parliament. He came third, behind Labour and the Conservatives, a result that was probably decisive in his own view of his political future. It looked like time to move on.

That it was not a moment too soon was clearly the view held by Dafydd Wigley. In her book on post war Plaid Cymru, Laura McAllister writes of the effect on Wigley of the Dafydd El presidency, saying: "There is no doubt he was unsuited for a place on the sidelines". If there were a Booker prize for understatement, that remark would be a runaway winner. There's no doubt that, beside his own temperamental inability to stay in the background, Wigley was hostile to Dafydd El's style and the nature of many of his ideas. Wigley is essentially a meat and two veg practical politician, while his successor was much more a *blanquette de veau* kind of guy. Perhaps just as important was the Stakhanovite Wigley's dim view of anyone who didn't work as hard as he did, which was very hard indeed.

Laura McAllister continues: "This period was an exasperating one for Wigley. 'I became more and more frustrated... so much so I seriously considered a career outside politics'... he didn't believe the party was addressing issues of concern or campaigning on them." In a crisp aside McAllister adds: "A more detached appraisal might say that, under Dafydd Elis Thomas, Plaid Cymru was not campaigning in the way Wigley understood political campaigning".

A detached observer might also consider that this *imbroglio* was resolved in a manner that not only suited the two participants but also satisfyingly reflected their contrasting characters. Dafydd El stepped aside and, in 1991, Wigley was restored to the presidency, the role in which he was clearly happiest. His predecessor proceeded to remodel himself. He resigned from Parliament at the 1992 election and emerged, to considerable public surprise, as a member of the House of Lords. There was astonishment among senior figures in Plaid Cymru who had been under the impression that a deal had been struck under which any peerage the party was offered would be taken up by someone else entirely. In a characteristic move Dafydd El had by-passed that arrangement and done his own fixing via a senior Welsh Conservative. Shortly after that he became a *quangoist*, as Chairman of the Welsh Language Board. This could hardly be described as the career choice of an obsessive moderniser (or, indeed, Marxist) but it nevertheless fulfilled the destiny privately wished by many Welsh mothers for their sons, a 'cushy job'. At the same time you can't help admiring the ability of both these Dafydds to arrange life in ways that were so much in harmony with their temperaments and ambitions.

You might wonder why, however, if matters had been disposed of in a way that appeared to be so satisfactory all round, there persisted between the two men a rift that was to play a decisive part in the fortunes of Plaid Cymru. It was part of the mood music of the party over the succeeding years, not all that intrusive perhaps, but as recognisably present as the Vivaldi that tinkles out of the loudspeaker in the hotel lift. The two men's careers were taking them in different directions. Wigley was doing what he liked best, running Plaid Cymru. Dafydd El, quango and peerage tucked under his arm, was a familiar, convivial figure in public life, in the arts world most obviously, by no means out of politics, but standing a little to one side of the rough and tumble of office; not for good, perhaps, but for the time being anyway. Later he was to become a key figure in Welsh politics once again and it was then, getting on for a decade after the presidency had changed hands for the second time, that this troubled relationship became a vital influence on the party's political future.

The results of the first elections to the National Assembly, in May 1999, had Plaid Cymru members delirious with excitement. It seemed that at last, after false starts, especially in local government, their dream of becoming an alternative to Labour could be on the verge of being realised. They had won 17 seats out of 60 and were clearly established as the main opposition in Cardiff Bay. More than that, though, they'd won Islwyn (the seat long held at Westminster by Neil Kinnock) Llanelli, and Rhondda, places in which the Labour legend had been forged. They had four seats at Westminster and two out of five in the European parliament. Who could blame them for believing the clear evidence that the Labour permafrost that had for so long covered much of Wales was at last melting?

Dafydd Wigley, at the height of his political powers and experience, was at the centre of all this. He was both the MP and AM for Caernarfon. He was the President of Plaid Cymru as well as being the party's leader in the National Assembly. He could justifiably take a lot of the credit for Plaid Cymru's unexpectedly successful performance at the election. He was, in one of those ominous adjectives of the political world, unassailable. Twelve months later, he was no longer his party's president nor its assembly leader. Twelve months further on he was no longer an MP. Another two years after that and he had left the assembly and floated instead in a political void illuminated mainly by the increasingly incandescent fury of his resentment. In its way it was a reversal of fortune lifted from the classics.

To a considerable extent this precipitous decline was down, once again, to chance. At the end of 1999 Wigley had an operation for a heart condition. Despite his taking a break from leading the party it became clear that he needed to reduce his work load. It was obvious to him and his colleagues that he was attempting more than even a fully fit man might realistically be expected to accomplish. A tricky decision had to be made between giving up his seat at Westminster, which would have meant a problematical by-election, or the party presidency. In the end he left the presidency and the assembly leadership, jobs in which he was succeeded, by a large majority, by Ieuan Wyn Jones.

Two elements in this decision became clear only later. One was an echo of Harold Macmillan's decision to resign as Prime Minister in October 1963, taken in hospital when he believed his condition was worse than it really was. In a similar way Wigley, who had been warned by his doctor that one consequence of surgery could be a temporary loss of confidence, might have made a precipitate decision. Certainly the robust health to which he was later restored suggested as much. At the same time, though, it would be wrong to ignore the fact that even the most successful leader has plenty of disaffected people around him; there are always those who have failed to get what they consider to be deserved preferment. Nor did they necessarily appreciate what some of them felt was the less than inclusive atmosphere that surrounded the driven and decisive Wigley. He had too many of the levers of power in his hands, some people believed, and too many duties to attend to in different parts of the country. Anyway, it's in the nature of politicians to seek change that might, in some undefined manner, bring them advantage. The longer a leader goes on, the more restless some elements of his party become and the greater grows the very human, if unfocused, desire for novelty. Margaret Thatcher and Tony Blair were two other leaders who felt the fierce pressure of other people's impatience with the status quo. There was certainly an element of that, too, in the fall of Charles Kennedy. In these circumstances any sign of physical frailty (Tony Blair's minor heart troubles, for example) is seized on as evidence of political mortality. There's no doubt that at this period Wigley had perceptibly less zest for the grinding machinery of politics, in his case operated weekly on an exhausting triangular route connecting Caernarfon, Westminster and Cardiff.

All those considerations and influences are easy enough to understand. But soon enough what looked like a routine and rational way of dealing with an easily-understood problem had been elevated to one of the most familiar devices of the political theatre: a plot. Not only that, but a plot that had its roots in the long and familiar rivalry between Plaid Cymru's two outstanding figures.

It's at this point that we enter that insubstantial world of rumour, speculation, gossip, misunderstanding, jealousy, mischief, accident, misinterpretation and circumstantial evidence in which a great deal of political activity takes place. One of the less well-appreciated facts about the creation of new institutions like the National Assembly is the scope they offer for intrigue. Politicians are thrown together all day, and sometimes at night, as some of them, far from home, have to hang around Cardiff waiting to perform their democratic duties two or three days a week. In these circumstances rumours are produced on an industrial scale. When it comes to plots, even those who are supposed to be most intimately involved don't always seem to be certain about what went on, whether incidents took place as described or, for that matter, whether they occurred at all.

One of the vogue words of modern politics is narrative, the process in which events and ideas unfold as some kind of coherent story with a logic that can be grasped even by the least alert voter. The point is that it has to make sense and carry the reader or the listener with it. In many ways it doesn't really matter if it is entirely accurate or not, as long as it isn't demonstrably unreliable, because what people believe to be true has as great an influence on them as what actually is true. So the narrative of Dafydd Wigley's resignation as Plaid Cymru's president and its aftermath obeys that rule because it makes its own kind of internal sense, even if it is impossible to say with any conviction where it might diverge from real life. What follows is what people say happened although, since some parts of it are mutually exclusive, it can't all be right.

One of those who urged Wigley to find a way of cutting his workload was Ieuan Wyn Jones, the man who was to succeed him as party president and, *ex officio*, as leader in the assembly. As time went on so Ieuan Wyn's role took on a more sinister aspect in the eyes of Wigley supporters. He had long been associated with Dafydd Elis Thomas and, indeed, was seen as being to some extent the presiding officer's protégé. More than that, even, since Dafydd El's role in the assembly meant that he had to keep an official distance from party matters, Ieuan Wyn was talked of by some people as being an essential component in his longer-term ambitions. The theory was that Dafydd El believed that, after the 2003 elections, Plaid Cymru would make further electoral gains and would force its way into the new administration that would be formed. His plan was to be in a position to take on a senior ministerial job, something that would be more easily facilitated if his ally, Ieuan Wyn, was leading Plaid Cymru.

So far, so Machiavellian, you might say and, while I make no claims for the truth or otherwise of such speculation, there's no doubt that Wigley's relationship with Ieuan Wyn deteriorated sharply. He came to feel that he had somehow been pushed from the presidency and that, even as a senior member of the assembly, he was being marginalised. Relationships between him and his successor were soon enough being described as 'pretty formal'.

Well, Wigley is, as I've said already, an emotional man, unsuited to second billing, never mind a walk-on part. He likes his name above the title. He began to think about another career, as he had a decade previously, perhaps in quangoland. The chairmanship of the Welsh Development Agency, then vacant, might have been just the thing, but his credentials probably weren't strong enough (he'd been out of industrial life for the best part of thirty years) and the Labour Party, which likes whenever possible to promote Labour people, was less than enthusiastic about the idea. The market for superannuated politicians was, in any case, on the slide. By the end of the year he had decided not to stand for the assembly at the next election. It's impossible to escape the sense that, if he'd felt loved, he might have stayed, but his settled view was that there was a conspiracy against him, something strongly denied by other people who were intimately involved in the running of the party at that time. The problem for Plaid Cymru was that, whether the conspiracy was real or not, its rumoured existence divided further an increasingly troubled organisation. The failure of the spectacular advances of the 1999 assembly elections to be mirrored by progress in the 2001 general election with the loss of Ynys Môn, began to provoke an itch of regret. Once again there was a sense of unfinished business. Perhaps, some people began to speculate, Wigley could make a comeback, somehow he could even be restored to the leadership. This was another familiar resort of nostalgic politicians and, when Michael Foot was leader of the Labour Party, similar rumours went round about Jim Callaghan.

In Wigley's case, though, it was perhaps a little more realistic to think he could turn back on the road to oblivion. He'd given up Caernarfon but there were still the regional list seats. What about something in South Wales? After all, he'd once worked in Merthyr Tydfil and been a member of the town council there. The *Western Mail* reported that he was considering it. It was immediately denied on Wigley's behalf although it was perfectly clear that he'd started the rumour himself, to see how it would play. What about North Wales, then? In the end, nothing doing.

Wigley has absolutely no talent for concealing his views, and while these stories might have looked like the kind of casual speculation or wishful thinking much enjoyed by politicians and their interpreters, it became clear that he thought that, somehow, he might have stayed in the mainstream and that he had been prevented from doing so by enemies within the party. Far from just muttering about this privately, immediately after the 2003 election he told the *North Wales Herald* exactly what he thought.

When approached about standing on the regional list for north Wales, he said, he had considered it seriously because friends and supporters had brought the matter up. However, he went on: "It became very clear that the party leadership did not want me to do that... The reason the party leadership gave me for not wanting me to stand was that they felt that I would undermine Ieuan Wyn Jones, the exact same reasons behind my reasons for not staying on in the Caernarfon constituency."

The intricacies of this dispute needn't detain us for too long since their chief importance lies in the effect they had on the mood within Plaid Cymru. The important point was that Wigley supporters were hardly being urged by him to fall in loyally behind their new leader, someone now being held responsible for the party's loss of seats at the election. If Wigley had still been in charge, his supporters believed, this comparative electoral disaster wouldn't have happened. In fact there were a number of other reasons, unconnected with leadership, why you might have expected this kind of result, not least the Labour Party waking up and putting a bit more effort into seats it had previously held for generations. But Plaid's expectations were pitched too high and Ieuan Wyn Jones carried the can. In this febrile atmosphere discontented people were likely to be suspected of plotting even if they were doing nothing of the kind. So it was that Ieuan Wyn decided to jump over the side of the *SS Plaid*, only to clamber back on board a few months later, dripping wet but otherwise largely unharmed.*

---

* Early in 2006, in a typically inscrutable move, it was announced that Ieuan Wyn had once again become the overall leader of Plaid Cymru, although he was not called president. A little later, in March 2006, Wigley announced, to much party and press

It's evident that the outcome of this critical time within Plaid Cymru can be put down both to the interplay of personal relationships over many years combined with more than an element of over-excitement when confronted with the idea that the party might actually reach a position in which it could exercise power in some way. Such a prospect was dealt a severe blow by the excursions that followed the 2003 election. Publicly divided parties pay the price for their divisions and, when it was suggested to one senior figure that these unseemly conflicts might set Plaid back by as much as four years, he replied sourly: "More like ten". Yet even the distant prospect of real influence had set some mature hearts fluttering so tremulously that thoughts arose about how the party might somehow be rescued from this dilapidated condition. Could the narrative be given another theatrical twist?

★

In the summer of 2005 rumours began to circulate about a rearrangement of the leadership of Plaid Cymru. Essentially the plan was that, some time in the following year, Dafydd Elis Thomas would step down from the presiding officer's chair and assume the leadership of his party in the National Assembly. Newly invigorated by a charismatic and experienced figurehead, the idea was, the party would not only recover lost ground but move forward once again. It would be a last, desperate throw of the political dice, but these were circumstances that demanded nerve above all other things. It was emphasised that this would not be a coup, but that it would take place with the agreement of Ieuan

---

acclaim, that he would be a candidate for a place on the North Wales list and hoped to win a seat in the assembly by this route. He had been urged by supporters to take option of standing in South Wales Central where he would have been almost certain to be returned, but he rejected the plan on the grounds that it was important for him to give his weight to the North Wales dimension of affairs, something he thought had been dangerously neglected by the national assembly. His decision almost certainly meant that he would fail to be elected. This time his story was that he had stood down in 2003 because he had believed he needed to give Ieuan Wyn Jones space to grow into the job. No reference was made to his previous well-known and entirely contradictory views. The overall result of these interventions was that, after getting on for three years of feuding, personal vendettas, plotting and sulking, Plaid Cymru had managed to restore itself to the position it had been in three years previously except that Wigley was now being officially described as a great man and a central figure in the effort to reverse the party's electoral decline.

Wyn, who would voluntarily step aside. The settled view was that while Ieuan Wyn was a hard-working and capable operator of the political machine, he didn't have the visionary talents of both his predecessors. What Ieuan Wyn lacked above all, many people felt, was the essential political attribute of charm. Well, that's obviously not a crime in politics, but it's a considerable handicap in someone who leads a small party and so lacks alternative elements of political magnetism, like patronage. In public Ieuan Wyn always appeared to be put out about something; even his attempts at light-hearted moments were unconvincing. That probably put him in the majority down at the National Assembly but, in contrast, deficiency in the charm department certainly wasn't something of which you could convincingly accuse Dafydd El.

Anyway, these rumours had all the more force because they clearly originated from Dafydd El himself, but, while no one doubted his abilities as a politician with an original cast of mind, it was soon evident that he had over-estimated his appeal to the party at large. When Plaid Cymru held its annual conference in September, accompanied by lots of press speculation about the idea of a new alignment in the party's leadership, it quickly became clear that large numbers of people wouldn't wear him at any price. Those who could broadly be described as the traditionalists viewed him with grave suspicion. They didn't like his views, his manner or his history. They didn't like him being a lord and the distance, real or imagined, it put between him and them. That distance was unavoidably emphasised by his role as Presiding Officer, but that increased the resentment at what was seen as the presumption that he could now pop along and save the party. And this from a man who looked to them like an ex-revolutionary turned member of the British establishment. All in all it became obvious that even more desperate measures were necessary. Those measures turned out to be quite extraordinary. Peace broke out.

Reports began to come in about unexpected alliances. Dafydd Wigley was seen at the opera with his arm around Dafydd Elis Thomas's shoulders. After years of frost, Wigley and Ieuan Wyn began to exchange phone calls and have meetings. Cynog Dafis, the former MP and Assembly Member, wrote about his abiding regret that he had been one of the people who had advised Wigley, in 2000, to think about standing down. Indeed, he was considered to be a close ally of Ieuan Wyn with whom he had gone to see

Wigley to make this suggestion. (His version was that they had
only intended him to cut his work load by relinquishing his leadership of the group in the assembly.) Now, however, he argued
that Wigley should return to the assembly in 2007, "in a leadership
role". Something very strange had come over these people who
had spent so much of their time in previous years embroiled in
disputes within their party.

What had overwhelmed them, it seemed, was the sense that
their personal opportunities to make a difference to Wales were
slipping away. Wigley, born 1943, Dafydd El, 1946, and Ieuan
Wyn, 1949, were all aware that failure to make some stupendous
advance at the next assembly elections, in 2007, would mean the
end of their careers, even on the small stage offered by Wales.
Cynog, born 1938, was lending a hand in what began to look like
Saga politics. This was no time for hanging about. What it all
implied in both practical and philosophical terms was spelt out
most clearly by Wigley in an article he wrote for the Plaid Cymru
paper, *Triban Coch*, in August 2005. Its most important assertion
was this: "Plaid Cymru exists not as a national dream tank, devis-
ing wish-lists for a perfect Wales". And the key question: "How
can we catch the people's imagination when we are tinkering with
the minutiae of policy?"

Then he came to the central issue, a dislocation in terms of Plaid
Cymru's history and revolutionary in relation to the aspirations so
long pursued by the traditionalist wing of the party, to whom he had
long been some kind of figurehead. In the National Assembly,
Wigley wrote, "the party has to decide whether it sees itself as basi-
cally oppositionalist, preserving a 'gold standard' for commitment to
Wales against which it can measure and criticise other parties as
they fall short. Alternatively it can see itself as a party of government
– whether that is by dint of an overall majority (unlikely with the
current electoral system) or as a party prepared, on certain terms, to
participate in partnership government."

The article went on to consider the consequences of Plaid
Cymru winning a majority at the 2007 election. Since this was a
result only slightly more likely than Elvis leading them to that
victory, Wigley arrived at the vital issue that all parties seriously
contemplating power must address: what should they tell the
voters? That's to say, what should they put in the manifesto. It
must be, he emphasised, a practical, costed programme but there

was even more to it than that. "The construction of such a manifesto will need to take on board at least two different contexts – what can be implemented as an overall majority government; and what the party could hope to implement if it is the largest party leading a partnership government. Some might argue that the manifesto should have a third section – what the party would like to do if we had full law-making, tax-varying and international treaty-making ability. But such a section might be seen as at best irrelevant and, at worst, confusing for the voter. It would be a hostage to fortune and used against us by political opponents."*

In a way that statement was, in itself, a kind of manifesto, combined with a tactical manual. And this is where the real trouble comes in. For years Plaid Cymru writhed on the hook of whether it believed in independence for Wales. When it said it didn't, its opponents accused it of concealing its true objectives. When it said it did, the same opponents said: "There we are, that's what they believed in all along but they were trying to hide it from the voters." As things stand now, the party does believe that Wales should have a parliament with law-making, tax-varying, treaty-making powers. Not to mention these matters would simply bring accusations that it was dissembling. To mention them, on the other hand, would indeed provide the hostage to fortune Wigley described.

People who understand the electoral system that governs the assembly think it is fanciful to imagine that Plaid Cymru could get anywhere near the overall majority that would allow it the freedom to govern as it chose. Frankly, if Labour can't manage that feat then no other party in Wales is going to do so in the foreseeable future. There was all the more reason, then, for Plaid to make the necessary adjustments to its public pronouncements that would allow it to serve in a coalition (for which 'partnership' is the user-friendly weasel word) with other parties, in all probability both the Liberal Democrats and the Tories. After all, as I've already described, that's what they started practising for in 2005. Will anything of this kind ever happen on a more formal basis? The best guess has to be almost certainly not, not least because a large section of the party itself would be outraged at the idea of

---

* Plaid Cymru had been much mocked over the years, for example, by its official ambition to get Wales into the United Nations, occupying, as Cymru, the seat next to Cuba.

abandoning the purity of their nationalist position and all the baggage that goes with it. The only thing the three opposition parties agree on is that they don't like Labour, which is hardly a programme for government. But the only way they can get any power is by acting together, even though they despise each other. At the same time for Plaid Cymru (and to a lesser extent the Liberal Democrats) to climb into bed with the Tories could well wreck the party for ever.

Nevertheless there's a significance in the fact that such a scheme is being put forward at all, and being put forward by people whose length and quality of service demands that they should be taken seriously. That doesn't lie so much in the fact that Plaid Cymru could crack up over it, although that shouldn't be ruled out, but that it reflects the central dilemma of all modern British political parties: what are the immutable ideas for which they stand? To what extent should those ideas be modified or abandoned if they are an obstacle to access to the power to put them into effect? Can you keep yourself warm at night by hugging your principles while your opponents dance round the bonfire they've made of their own? Perhaps the choice for a contemporary political party now has become similar to one between Cavaliers and Roundheads made in Sellars and Yeatman's imperishable *1066 and All That:* Wrong but Wromantic against Right but Repulsive.

The Labour Party has answered such questions in the most spectacular way. The Conservatives would like to do it and are moving in that direction through the unexpected election of David Cameron as leader, even if it's not yet clear quite how they might manage it. That's not least because of their difficulty in deciding precisely what a twenty-first century Conservative should distinctively stand for. The Liberal Democrats, also divided into modernisers (in this case known as the Orange Book faction) and traditionalists, argue with each other over the health service, privatisation, economic policy and Europe among other things, and puzzle over the adjustments necessary to reach that state of grace known as electability.

The story of Plaid Cymru in the first years of the National Assembly for Wales tells us a great deal about the nature of contemporary British politics, the dilemmas that confront the parties and the similar ways in which they tackle them. If you dig a little you can seen that the parties in the National Assembly aren't divided by any deep questions of principle. Plaid Cymru and the Liberal Democrats, and to a considerable extent the Conservatives, don't seriously disagree with the general direction taken by the Welsh Assembly Government. On issues like the health service, education and industrial development, the assembly's most vital responsibilities, by and large they don't argue that they'd do things differently, just that they'd do them better. Nor do they devote much time to the one distinctive Welsh issue that has long been a matter of fierce controversy: the Welsh language. They understand very well that to make this a central theme of political debate would at best arouse deep suspicions in a country where the practical truth is that 80 per cent of the population doesn't speak Welsh and of whom a substantial proportion are either indifferent to its fate or suspicious of its promotion. Their number includes, despite the cultural inclusiveness they like to exude, some Labour MPs.

The curious, paradoxical thing about devolution is not that it's made Wales more distinct from the rest of the United Kingdom but that it's made it more the same. In an unexpected, unplanned way, it might turn out to have dished the nats after all.

UNCOMMON LAW

THERE'S A GREAT DEAL OF quiet pleasure to be gained from one unintended consequence that arose from Britain's last great industrial battle, fought out with such unswerving dedication by Margaret Thatcher and Arthur Scargill. During her premiership Mrs Thatcher devoted almost no time at all to advancing the cause of women in politics. In her eleven years as Prime Minister only one woman, Janet Young, Baroness Young of Farnworth, served in her Cabinet and did so only briefly. On the other side, when it came to questions of gender equality, the National Union of Mineworkers had a reputation for being one of the most reactionary organisations in the western world. When the long strike was over, though, and as the smoke cleared, we could see in the old industrial areas that women, who had played such a substantial part in campaigning for the miners and often stiffening their resolve, were now about to take on a new and significant role in public life. They had marched out of the kitchen and, despite the grumblings of many men, they had no intention of resuming their domestic anonymity.

It's impossible not to savour this unexpected turn of events, even though it is to a large extent a mistaken account of what actually took place. It is now firmly established as part of the mythology of this period and, like many of the other myths that colour the story of the miners' strike, it is an ineradicable element of the way in which people describe that period and the influence it has on their behaviour. Of course there's no denying that there's been an arresting change, almost a revolution, in the growth of women's contribution to public life in the last couple of decades. In places like Wales the simple political arithmetic tells you almost as much as you need to know. In the period of almost eighty years between women first being permitted to stand for parliament and 1997, Wales managed to elect a total of four. In 2005 eight of them won seats at Westminster. And there might have been more if continuing arguments over discrimination hadn't taken an unexpectedly sensational course, which we'll come to later. In only the fifth year of the National Assembly for Wales, in the 2003 elections, thirty women and thirty men divided the seats between them.

These are remarkable statistics, but it would be wrong to think that the miners' strike somehow ignited a fuse that led to an explosion of emancipation, that until the mid-eighties most women in working-class areas had led lives of socially-imposed obscurity before suddenly leaping on to the public stage in an outburst of noise and colour. Some of them had been there long before. For example, in his account of the history of the South Wales miners between 1914 and 1926, Robin Page Arnot records this press report from October 16, 1926. "Mrs Elvira Bailey, an elderly woman, of High Street, Treorchy, was given two months for throwing a stone at P.C. Thos. McCullough. Rhondda Stipendiary (D. Lleufer Thomas): 'You threw the first stone at the P.C. and you set a very bad example to the women of the district. I find that women have been taking too prominent a part in these disturbances and I must impose a penalty that will be a deterrent to others.'"

Or there was Catherine Griffiths of Nantyffyllon who, when she died in March 1988, was described in her *Daily Telegraph* obituary as reputedly the last surviving suffragette. She was clearly both courageous and enterprising. "Her finest moment was perhaps when she stole into the chamber of the House of Commons and strewed tin tacks upon the seat of Lloyd George ('To make him sit up,' she later explained.) Subsequently she was gaoled for breaking into the House of Lords."

She trained as a nurse in Merthyr Tydfil and the views she formed of society in the early twentieth century would be echoed by other women long afterwards. "Working as a Queen's Jubilee Nurse (district nurse) in Merthyr and Cardiff she often had to deal with mining and docklands injuries. What she saw in the poor homes made her a radical and a suffragette. 'A woman was just a slave – there to attend to the needs of men,' she would recall."

Throwing stones and spreading tin tacks weren't the only ways in which women could hope to influence the establishment. Some of them could also join it, and share in the tremendous influence exercised by those great totalitarian institutions, the Labour-controlled councils, and the ripples of patronage that lapped out from them across entire counties. In the council chamber, in the party system, in the various committees that ran things like education, or up on the bench as Justices of the Peace, formidable women got their share of deference: women like Roy Jenkins's mother, Hattie.

On vacation from Oxford just before the War, Jenkins "drove into the centre of Pontypool to collect my mother from the Magistrates' Court and parked in the most convenient and there-fore most illegal-looking place. My companion was convinced that we were about to be removed, but when one or two constables passed they merely saluted. Then when a large officer decorated with the badges of a chief superintendent advanced and actually tapped on the window he thought his fears were about to be vindi-cated. But when I wound it down the police dignitary merely said: 'Your mother asked me to pop out and say that we are just finish-ing the last case, and she will be with you in ten minutes.'"

Jenkins then added ruefully, reflecting on his father's imprison-ment: "Perhaps they were all in a conspiracy to compensate for 1926." A more likely explanation is what Jenkins refers to as "a certain sense of local power", which recognises the daily reality of South Wales politics, around which sensible people were properly respectful of the arbitrary authority wielded by the councillor/commissar and various other apparatchiks of the Labour machine. Many years later, for example, contacting the leader of one county council involved telephoning the school where he worked. When the headmaster answered the phone you could hear a mixture of nervousness and urgency entering his voice as he promised to hurry off and get the man concerned. The councillor was the school caretaker but the headmaster was, in effect, his employee; there was no question about who was superior to whom.

Women, as we can see, were by no means entirely excluded from sharing in this kind of power, but for generations the ideal of mature Welsh womanhood took an entirely different shape. In creating this popular image there was perhaps no more potent influence than Richard Llewellyn's novel, *How Green Was My Valley* and, even more strongly, its 1941 Oscar-winning Hollywood version. It was this film more than any other that fixed the public identity of Welsh women for a lifetime. Above all the idea of the Welsh mam, compassionate and courageous, fierce in the interests of her family, clear-sighted about right and wrong, her arms some-times open in love, sometimes folded in grim disapproval.

How some of us laughed when we saw *How Green* for the first time, perhaps twenty years after it was made, as people with American accents talked in those backwards constructions that was often the outside world's version of how it believed the Welsh spoke English, in the few moments they took off from singing hymns as they tramped to and from the colliery. In fact this is pretty much how Richard Llewellyn wrote the book so it would be wrong in this case to talk of typical Hollywood distortion.

Twenty-five years after that, though, we might have paused to reflect on at least part of the story it told. There is a long strike, provoked by a wage cut, in which the five Morgan sons, union activists, leave their home because their father goes on working. He accuses them of talking 'socialist nonsense'.

One night, because of the strikers' hostility to her husband Gwilym, Beth Morgan, (in the book called Mama rather than Mam) goes out into the hills to confront them. "If harm do come to my Gwilym," she says, "I will find out the men and I will kill them with my hands. And that I will swear by God Almighty. And there will be no Hell for me. Nobody will go to Hell for killing lice."

Of course there were wagonloads of clichés and sentimentality carted into the fictionalised South Wales village John Ford had built in the hills of Malibu. Nevertheless, in terms of the kind of the emotional arguments that were woven through industrial life during much of the twentieth century, *How Green Was My Valley* tells a story that remains familiar, not least in the portrayal of the indomitable mam. As the narrator, Huw Morgan, looks back, he says: "If my father was the head of our house, my mother was its heart".

Yes, I know, that sentence might have many people in a modern audience looking for one of those stout paper bags provided by the airlines, but at the same time it carries within it a powerful image for a lot of Welsh people; not to mention a powerful image of what others believe Welsh people to be. Deirdre Beddoe, emeritus professor of Welsh Women's History at the University of Glamorgan, points out that, actually, it's not untrue. "There is an awful lot of truth in the tradition, mainly because for much of the twentieth century and certainly for the nineteenth century Welsh women were stay-at-home housewives and mothers. For most women there was no choice but to be a mam and run the home."

More than that, there was a view that work and marriage were incompatible occupations for able women. So much so that they were pretty well banned from combining the two. Deirdre Beddoe explains: "There were just two professions open to women – teaching and nursing – and both operated marriage bars. That meant that if you chose to be a teacher you had to take the veil. It was a choice between your career and home and family. And those marriage bars continued up till 1944."

Curiously enough, though, the institutionalised discrimination that blocked careers in one direction could sometimes provide the opportunity for women to carve out influential positions by another route. One of them, for example, was Mrs Rose Davies, known simply as Mrs Rose through the entire length of the Aberdare Valley and beyond. Born in 1882, the daughter of a tin worker, she'd made a career as a teacher (becoming an assistant school mistress at the age of eighteen) before being forced to abandon the profession when she married. But at the beginning of the twentieth century she'd become an activist in the Independent Labour Party and a close friend of its leader, Keir Hardie, who in 1900 became MP for Merthyr Tydfil. That constituency had two members because it also included Aberdare. The other was a Liberal, D.A. Thomas, the wealthy coalowner who later became Viscount Rhondda. In the succeeding years the Liberals were about to be overtaken by the Labour Party; Mrs Rose was one of those who, through a combination of personal vigour and political patronage, was to benefit from this political movement and wield awesome influence in education and local government. As Ursula Masson points out in her essay on Mrs Rose Davies in the *Dictionary of Labour Biography*, the marriage bar made talented and energetic people like her available for unpaid work in civil and political life.

Among other things she was the first woman to chair Glamorgan County Council, but in those days the great aldermanic figures of local government seemed to give off a glow of authority that extended well beyond their official positions. For decades in the Aberdare Valley anyone experiencing a difficulty with schools, or housing or health or any number of common problems was given a familiar piece of advice. "Have a word with Mrs Rose," someone would murmur, guiding the enquirer to what was widely believed to be the best source of knowledge and influence in the district, probably in the entire county of Glamorgan. She died in 1958, a month after collapsing on her way to yet another committee meeting. But even now, almost half a century

on, among older people in a district where memories are long, to
mention her name is more often than not to be answered with a
nod of recognition and a tone of respect: "Ah, yes, Mrs Rose".

It's worth remembering that Mrs Rose Davies was well into
her forties before all women actually got the vote. The first step, in
1918, had enfranchised women over thirty, but it wasn't until ten
years later that they qualified, like men, at the age of twenty-one.
And even if some well-connected women of character and determination could make a splash in the comparatively shallow waters
of local government, their prospects of a bigger career, at
Westminster for example, were very circumscribed. What people
like Mrs Rose were allowed to do, as were many after her, was to
put up a brave fight in a hopeless constituency and, safely
defeated, go home again. For reasons Ursula Masson is at a loss to
explain, she stood for parliament in 1929, in Honiton in Devon of
all unlikely places, where the victorious Conservative and the
second placed Liberal between them got more than 97 per cent of
the vote. Mrs Rose got 914 votes (the Tory got almost 18,000) and
never fought a Westminster seat again.

A similar thing happened to Ann Clwyd. In 1970, at the age of
33, she stood in Denbigh, her birthplace. "I was asked to stand
because it was a hopeless seat. It was one with a very big
Conservative majority. We had a very good result in that election.
I think it was the only constituency in Britain where there was a
one per cent swing to Labour. After that people said, 'Oh, it's
going to be easy for you from now on. People are going to be offer-
ing you seats.' But, of course, that's not how it works. I can
remember Jill Foot saying to Michael, 'Michael, can't you find Ann
a seat?' And of course that wasn't how it worked, although it did
help to be part of the old boy network."

At that time Ann Clwyd was the Welsh correspondent of the
Guardian, ambitious, sharp, young, petite, blonde, pretty and smart.
In other words entirely unsuitable for selection as a Labour candidate in a seat where she might actually be in danger of winning. At
the 1974 election she fought Gloucester where people took one
glance at her denim suit and said, "Well, you don't look like an MP".

In that same year she'd tried for the nomination in the Cynon
Valley (as the Aberdare constituency had now become known) but
was rejected. Ten years later, when the sitting MP died suddenly,
she tried again, now with a *CV* packed with virtually every public

service credential a Labour candidate could stack up, including five years in the European Parliament, of which she was still a member at that time. She was selected. Afterwards, she later recalled, a member of the constituency party told her she hadn't been selected on the previous occasion because she wore the wrong clothes. "And I said, 'What do you mean?' And they said, 'You had a bright green jacket and white trousers on'."

So there we were. In 1984, only eighty-odd years after Keir Hardie had become Wales's first Labour MP, not much less than that since Mrs Rose Davies had joined the ILP in the same place, Ann Clwyd became the first woman to represent a Welsh mining seat. She was, too, only the fourth woman to represent any Welsh constituency. Two of the other three had had outstanding advantages. In 1929, Megan Lloyd George won Anglesey for the Liberals but, after all, she was the daughter of the former Prime Minister, David Lloyd George. In 1950 Flint was won for Labour by Mrs Eirene White (later Baroness White of Rhymney). She happened to be the daughter of that contradiction in terms, a famous civil servant, Dr Thomas Jones, who served as assistant, then deputy, secretary to the Cabinet for fourteen years, six of them during Lloyd George's premiership. Any old boy network of which Ann Clwyd might become an associate member couldn't really compete with such an accumulation of influence.*

In fact, though, despite the reputation the NUM might have had for male chauvinism, she says that she always found many union leaders supportive, in particular Emlyn Williams and Dai Francis, the president and General Secretary of the South Wales miners. It was the case, too, that the first person to sign her nomination papers in the Cynon Valley was an NUM official. That she was elected when the miners' strike was already under way (the by-election was in May 1984) is, too, an indication of how attitudes were already being realigned. Once again it's possible to see that the events of 1984-85 revealed social shifts more than they created them.

Hywel Francis says there's no doubt that, while there was a kind of social revolution, there's a danger of exaggerating its impact. "In

---

* The third Welsh woman MP, Mrs. (later Dame) Dorothy Rees, was the Labour MP for Barry in the brief period between the general elections of February 1950 and October 1951.

my experience in the Dulais Valley large numbers of women were not *just* miners' wives, as they were described. They were nurses and teachers and had lives of their own outside the home, outside their domestic responsibilities. They were active trade unionists.

"Many women had more experience than the miners themselves in organising their workplaces. The miners had inherited that legacy from previous generations. They hadn't had to fight to organise their workplaces. But very often factory workers or teachers had to do that themselves. Very often those women who emerged already had industrial and trade union experience."

That's not to say that there weren't doubts and misgivings, a sense that a familiar social order was shifting under their feet. After all, the strike was about saving a traditional, and pretty well exclusively male, industry. If that went, what else might go with it? As Hywel Francis recalls, for some people it was something that nagged away at the idea of what their lives were and what they might become.

"I chaired the Neath, Dulais and Swansea Valley miners' support group. We would have a meeting every Sunday evening which was obviously about the matter of food distribution which was largely organised by the women, certainly led by the women. But there'd be political discussions in these meetings about the role of women then and in the future.

"Older miners who were retired but who were there supporting would often be antagonistic to using some of the funds we had to allow those women to go campaigning or to go on picket lines or to London to speak. And it came to a crisis when we in the Dulais Valley were rather exotically linked to the London Gays and Lesbians miners' support group. They wanted to buy a £5,000 mini bus for the women, to allow them to campaign. But we didn't know how to do this so we had to ensure they wrote a letter saying they were already buying it because if we had been given the £5,000 I think it would have been vetoed. I think the older men would have said the task of the women was to ensure there was food in the bellies of their children and clothes on their backs."*

---

*The extent to which attitudes have changed on some of these matters is indicated by the fact that in the Rhondda, where wearing a pink shirt could plunge a man into sexual controversy, the constituency's Labour MP sent his own picture, wearing only his underpants, to a gay website. While the newspapers tried to whip up outrage for a time, the furore, such as it was, didn't last long.

This ambiguity is also reflected by Deirdre Beddoe in her book on Welsh women's history, *Out of the Shadows*, in which she writes: "In many valleys the strike brought a new respect for women. In other places men felt threatened by this new demonstration of women's power. At Markham, in the Sirhowy Valley, the men refused to allow women on to the picket lines, so the women split off and continued raising funds and collecting food."

In an interview she told me that she believed that 84-85 differed in one important respect from what had gone before. "I think that women are much, much more visible. They are not only running soup kitchens, although they did that, they are not only collecting food and money and organising finances and loans for people. They did all that but now they are on public platforms, they're alongside Arthur Scargill, they're at the head of marches with the banners and, of course, the media takes the whole issue up. They're there, they're visible, they're in the front row. It was said at the time, 'We're not behind the men, this time we're along-side them'. So I think the visibility thing is very important."

The point perhaps is this. Women weren't second-class domestic supporters for men one minute and the next throwing off their pinnies and elbowing them aside on the picket line and at the barricades. This entire world was changing; the decline of heavy industry all around Britain and the new structure of employment meant women were assuming a different role whether they liked it – and whether men liked it – or not. So, for example, they had spontaneously created one notable political campaign. It was women from Wales who, in 1981, took up the cause against American cruise missiles being based on British soil. The march they organised led to the establishment of the women's peace camp at Greenham Common in Berkshire, and inspired a protest that lasted for a decade.

That long campaign, though, was specifically organised by and for women. What happened during the miners' strike was that women asserted equality in what had traditionally been, in industries like mining, a largely male preserve of protest. In its turn this recast role was to have considerable political consequences in the succeeding decades.

"I don't think this strike and its impact on women came out of nowhere," Deirdre Beddoe says. "But I think it pushed women forward. It's like a jolt in the progress of women. The strike gave women a lot of confidence. It made them realise that if they wanted to change things, if they wanted to fight things, they needed access to power for themselves. I think there are long-term consequences of that, of women realising they needed the power to protest, to save their own communities."

Siân James was one of the women who stepped onto the front line of industrial and political activism during the strike. It wasn't a premeditated decision but a product of chance and, it's clear, the sheer length of that strike. To a great extent it was impossible to hide from it. "It started off in a traditional way," she said. "I always say that I don't think there was a miner in that strike who had to stand at the door and tell the rent man that he wasn't going to be paid that week. My husband certainly didn't do that. He wasn't the person either who had to phone the electricity board up to say that there wasn't the money to pay them. Or go down to the school to say that I didn't have the week's dinner money to pay."

As the strike wound on through 1984 so there was more to do, organising food parcels, collecting money, arranging raffles. "I had a little scam going which my mother supported. She grew plants and I sold them door to door. And there was nothing we weren't prepared to do. We once raffled the same table top organ six times because no one wanted it."

Terry Thomas, at that time vice president of the South Wales miners, points out that there was nothing new in women campaigning during a strike. They had done so in 1972 and in 1974 but the difference was that on those occasions they had done so on their own.

"Their determination was even stronger than some members of the NUM," he says. "Coming up to the end of the strike you actually had women arguing against their husbands going back to work. The work that they did, not just supporting their husbands or their fathers or their brothers or neighbours who were on strike, but alongside the men on the picket lines. They went out to address meetings. Women who had never stood on their feet to address a meeting. It was amazing the way they came forward."

Siân James was twenty-four years old when the strike began, the wife, daughter, daughter-in-law and sister of miners. One Sunday afternoon at the Dulais Valley support group there was a call for someone to speak at a meeting in London the next day.

"I said, 'Right, I'll do it'. I went home and said to my husband:

'You'll have to have the children tomorrow. I'm going to London. Hafina and I are going to London and we're going to do public speaking.' We weren't too certain about what the public speaking would entail, but we were going to do it."

The campaign soon drew women more deeply into the wider political debate that provided its context. It was, for example, a logical extension of the arguments over coal to consider the matter of nuclear energy. Some of the men, Siân James says, would complain that this wasn't really what their activities were meant to be about.

"They would tell me: 'My wife isn't interested in all this'. And I'd say: 'I'm sure she is. Have you asked her?' And they'd say: 'Hmm.' And you knew that their wives were. And we'd have some cracking debates on whether it was right to read the *Sun* and whether Page Three was acceptable, and it really did open a much wider world to a lot of us. We once had a very lively discussion on whether sugar was a luxury or a necessity. All the women argued that it was a luxury and all the men thought it was a necessity."

This was the experience of someone who had left school at sixteen with no more pressing aspiration than that of getting married, which she did more or less immediately. She had her first child at the age of seventeen and another before she was twenty. Work? Well, she says, girls from her area often talked about the inspiring choice they had – between a job in the cardboard box factory or one in the cigar factory. But it's important not to jump to the conclusion that this was yet another unmotivated, somewhat bolshy, nineteen-seventies teenager willing to take whichever route through life that was the least challenging. She might have been discovered by the strike but, it's clear, if that hadn't swept her to the front something else would have.

Not least because she came from an intensely political family. "In our house everything stopped every night in time for us all to watch the Nine o'clock News." Her mother was a passionate advocate of asking difficult questions and challenging authority. If teachers didn't seem up to the mark in some way the young Siân was urged to remind them that they were paid out of public money. She was particularly intense on issues connected with the Welsh language. If the post office didn't have a Welsh version of some form or other, her mother would stand there and demand that it should be made available. "My father would say, 'Don't make a fuss today'."

That account endorses Deirdre Beddoe's view that the crucial change in the role of women wasn't one of attitude but of visibility. And in that way there's no doubt that the strike affected the future course of Siân James's life. But she was clearly someone ready to seize a fresh opportunity, finding the stage on which she could flourish. "On the day they announced the strike was ending, that the men would be going back to work on the following Tuesday, we were all very angry, we were all crying, but my mother said to me, 'You didn't want this strike to end'. In a way she was right. I wanted the misery to end but, really, I didn't want the rest of it to end."

And for her, in a sense, it didn't. She became a full-time university student in Swansea and, once she'd graduated, set out on a career that employed her talents as a campaigner, eventually becoming director of Welsh Women's Aid, an organisation chiefly concerned with providing help and protection for women and children who are victims of abuse. In her case the strike was an opportunity, if an unhappy one, to make a different life. For many of the other women who had worked alongside her it was to a great extent a self-contained event from which they could now turn back.

"I think that one of the tough things for the women who had been active was that some of them were quite happy and content to go back to doing what they'd been doing what they'd done before. Although it wasn't right for me and several of my friends you couldn't say to them: 'Oh, come on now, you've been liberated'. It was important to them and we felt we had to support that. But what I did know, and I took great heart from, was that those women were much more politically aware, were much better organised, and certainly less likely not to say their piece."

There was to be yet another step. In May 2005 she became the Labour MP for Swansea East. She was chosen from an all-women shortlist, a system of positive discrimination that to a substantial extent owed its existence to the changing social attitudes that emerged around the strike. By this stage, in Swansea at least, this selection wasn't a matter of public controversy, although there was plenty of resentment, sometimes expressed not so *sotto voce*. Her critics said initially she'd been shoehorned in as a Tony Blair loyalist. A few months later, when she voted against the proposal for ninety days detention for terrorist suspects, she was accused of disloyalty to the Blair government. She moved into the constituency and painted her front door bright red so that people would know where to knock if they ever wanted to speak to her about that or any other matter.

★

All women shortlists and, in the early days of the National
Assembly, a system of twinning constituencies, were the crowbar
with which the Labour Party opened up a route that allowed far
more women to take political office. What was surprising was the
speed and vigour with which it happened. This was not the traditional Labour way of doing things. In the old industrial areas it
was viewed as more or less revolutionary and was often fiercely
resented, not least because it was about more than the simple
question of who went to Westminster or Cardiff Bay. These were
places in which the definition of work had largely been man's
work and there was a strong tendency to shelter many aspects of
political life under that same roof. It went without saying that
women weren't barred from any office by any regulation or principle. Indeed, some of them achieved it. The fact was that there
had been some women MPs, a small number admittedly, and
other women who were a powerful presence in local government.
That could be offered as proof that there was no gender discrimination. It was a bit like one of those clubs that believe the
presence of a single Jewish member is irrefutable evidence that
they are entirely free of racial prejudice.

At the same time it would be a mistake to think that this was
an attitude confined to that unreformed world where the social
structure had been established by the economic arrangements of
the nineteenth century. Even in the leafy suburbs of Tory England
Conservative selection committees were known to have asked a
woman candidate: "What will your husband do for sex if you are
away at Westminster all week?" Breathtaking though that question
is, it reveals a deep anxiety about more than some kind of political
closed shop. It shows, too, the way in which people (women as well
as men, very often) watch uneasily as the familiar framework of
their cherished kind of society is dismantled piece by piece.

But in the movement of gender relationships, you begin to
wonder, is there a particular sensitivity involved in the advance of
women politicians? Does it also indicate a fear that, if selected,
women might not actually go round behaving like men? More
than that, that women in political life might introduce more than
an element of the unexpected. It's not that they're not up to the
job but that they might be inclined to dispense with some of the

traditional assumptions that have provided the tacitly agreed boundaries within which parties work.

That is exactly what Margaret Thatcher did. Her enthusiasm for presiding over an industrial revolution in Britain, especially in the public sector, and her absolute refusal to sentimentalise the miners and their history, was instrumental in breaking with the practices of her predecessors. Some, like Edward Heath, planned to do things differently but in the end lacked the necessary resolution. Another, Harold Macmillan, said as late as 1981: "There are three bodies no sensible man directly challenges: the Roman Catholic Church, the Brigade of Guards and the National Union of Mineworkers". In other words, three of the most suffocatingly male organisations in the entire world. And, of course, Macmillan said no sensible *man*.

Paradoxically though, despite Mrs Thatcher's bold political iconoclasm which brought her party a period of unprecedented success, she soon ceased to be an inspiration to her successors. Instead she became the equivalent of an ancestor whose fortunes were founded on the kind of enterprise which has now fallen into disrepute: gun-running, say, or the slave trade. In the upper reaches of the twenty-first century Conservative Party, tributes to her greatness became largely perfunctory and nobody dreamt of proposing that the party should follow her example in either style or policy. No one said: "It was wonderful under Maggie, let's try and do it all over again". Quite the reverse, indeed.

Maybe a substantial part of the reason is, as I've already suggested, because her self-belief, her relish of confrontation and her unwillingness to be bound by tradition do not belong in the conventional portrait of femininity favoured by the sound bite culture of public life. The handbag is already gathering dust in the military museum alongside the halberd and the broadsword. Let's not do what Margaret Thatcher did, the argument goes, let's do what Tony Blair did, in the process brushing aside Blair's undisguised admiration for Thatcher's achievement in dumping much of the Conservatives' inconvenient past.

Ann Clwyd, whose persistence finally got her to Westminster, is someone else who discovered the kind of expectations loaded on to women MPs. At the end of December 2003, an astonished *Observer* said of her: "She's the firebrand left-wing MP who stunned the Commons into silence when she backed Tony Blair over Iraq. Many said she saved the Prime Minister's skin." What she did was one of those very rare things in modern politics. She made a speech in the House of Commons that actually made a difference. But more than that, she did it in the face of the hostility of those who in the past would have been her natural allies.

In the Commons in February that year she had spoken with transparent emotion and considerable authority on the case for going to war against Saddam Hussein. Given her long association with the cause of the Iraqi Kurds, 25 years of travelling to the country, her commitment was unmistakeable. She'd even been sacked from the Opposition front bench because of it when, in 1995, the Labour Whips ordered her to return from northern Iraq where she was meeting people who'd been bombarded by Saddam's forces. Her refusal put an end to whatever hopes she might have had of conventional political advancement.

That kind of defiance in a humanitarian cause would have got plenty of support on the left of the Labour Party. What was to shock them was, when it came to a vital decision, the conclusion she drew from this deeply-felt experience. February 26, 2003, was the day on which the Commons was due a crucial vote on committing troops to the war. It might have been that the Prime Minister's future depended on the extent of the rebellion by Labour members.

Ann Clwyd got to her feet just before four o'clock in the afternoon, telling MPs that she had recently returned from two days travelling in Iraq. She described many of the things she had seen there and some of the accounts she had been given of the treatment of prisoners. "A former prisoner told me that a university professor gave birth at the Abu Ghraib prison while he was there. Apparently, because of the very poor diet of thin soup and bread, she did not have enough milk to feed the baby when it was born. She begged the guards for milk, but they refused to give it and the baby died. She held that baby in her arms for three days and would not give up the body. At the end of three days, because the temperature in the prison was very hot...the body began to smell. They took the woman and her dead baby away. I asked the former prisoner what happened to her and he said that she was killed...

"I say to my colleagues, please, who is to help the victims of Saddam Hussein's regime unless we do? I believe in regime change. I say that without hesitation, and I will support the Government tonight because I think they are doing a brave thing."

Commentators thought that the power of Ann Clwyd's

personal testimony had been enough to sway as many as thirty votes. As it was 139 Labour MPs voted against the Government but, it was suggested, that one speech had the effect of at least reducing the damage to a level that was sustainable. Two questions arise from this event. Were those who were moved by that speech influenced because it was made by a woman? Did those who deplored her endorsement of war, and there were many on her own side, do so with all the more vehemence for the same reason, that they felt it was an inappropriate sentiment for a woman to express? Did they get the same sense of unease as many did when Mrs Thatcher urged people to rejoice at the recapture of South Georgia in April 1982? And if they felt those things was it more because of an entrenched view of how women ought to think and behave rather than any careful weighing of the available evidence?

What these questions do is draw attention to the widely held but essentially mistaken belief that there is a class of person described as a woman politician who can be placed in a different category from any other politician who is not a woman. The idea sometimes put about, that they are unable to cope with what's described as 'Punch and Judy politics' does not bear even superficial examination in a world that contains people like Clare Short and Ann Widdecombe. On a local government trip to Strasbourg in the seventies I saw one well-known woman Labour councillor block the exit doors to the tarmac where the much delayed flight home was waiting. "Right," she called out with considerable authority and volume, "nobody leaves until we've all had our duty-frees." Many of those who have been prominent in the Labour Party have been extremely combative left-wingers, people like the Sheffield MP Joan Maynard who was widely known by the title of 'Stalin's granny'. It's patronising to say that women can't cope when the proper argument should be about whether politics should be conducted in a jeering, adversarial manner, whatever the proportions of men to women involved.

Barbara Castle was a left-winger too, in her day one of the most famous in the entire party, but she was also independent-minded enough to embrace what was seen as a right-wing policy and attempt to curb the powers of the trade unions. Nor did she have any of the self-doubt that is popularly supposed to give women politicians a sense of perspective often lacking in men. When she was sacked by Jim Callaghan when he became Prime

Minister in 1976 she wrote furiously in her diary: "I know – and have always known – that I am one of the best Ministers in this Government: and certainly the toughest fighter for our Party's policies. And I am at the peak of my powers."

Well over twenty years later, at the age of 90, almost blind and very deaf, she was still on public platforms, campaigning for pensioners and giving the Blair government the rough edge of her very fluent tongue. But Barbara Castle was a phenomenon because she formed part of a tiny minority. Her very prominence drew attention to the shortcomings of the system. The fact was that the most important aspect of the debate over women politicians didn't lie in any distinctive character they might have had, or their suitability for inclusion in the boarding school cum golf club atmosphere that for a long time characterised the House of Commons. What was fundamental was how many – or, rather, how few – of them there were. What they haven't done – and why should they? - is to introduce, or attempt to introduce, any kind of mumsy element into the way in which political life is conducted. It may be that Margaret Thatcher was rather more typical of women politicians than popular opinion has properly grasped.

Even after the 2005 general election women made up only 20 per cent of the membership of the House of Commons. Later that year the Equal Opportunities Commission calculated that it would take another two hundred years – or forty elections – for them to get to 50 per cent. So at the very least a mathematical injustice was clearly continuing, despite the fervently-expressed desires of party leaders to do something about it. In the Conservative Party contenders for the leadership peered nervously over the edge of the precipice of compulsion and drew back. We must do more, they said, without saying much about what more might actually mean. Perhaps their circumspection owed something to a calamity that had overtaken Labour.

*

In many aspects of life there is often a great gap between what people say they want and what they would really like to happen. Sometimes, as in the case of some members of the Labour Party, they don't necessarily see a connection between the two things. So while people don't publicly dissent from the view that there should be more women MPs, they can often find something to object to in the methods by which that object is achieved. That is certainly what occurred in Blaenau Gwent, in one of the most remarkable political episodes of recent times.

If you're going to have a spectacular row in the Labour Party it's difficult to think of anywhere much better to stage it than Blaenau Gwent, a constituency that, when it was known as Ebbw Vale, was represented for well over sixty years by two of the most famous men in twentieth century British politics, Aneurin Bevan and Michael Foot. They were intimate friends and allies until Bevan's death in 1960, when Foot succeeded him as the constituency's MP. They were two of the most brilliant performers in public life, compellingly articulate campaigners at the heart of the long and bitter conflicts that persistently divided Labour, but at the same time unswerving in their loyalty to their party. That loyalty was almost seamlessly represented within the constituency itself. Or it was until May 2005.

When Llew Smith, Michael Foot's successor as the MP, decided after the 2001 general election that he would not fight the seat again he was well aware that, if he waited until after November 2002 to make the formal announcement of his retirement, the party rules meant it would be compelled to select the next candidate from an all-women shortlist. His view was that there should be an open choice and therefore he made his intentions known in good time. It didn't make any difference, though, because the Labour Party decided that, in any case, there would be an all-women shortlist. The rules might not have said they had to have one, but the rules didn't say they *couldn't* have one.

In the constituency this was considered to be a pretty under-hand way of going on, not an unusual state of affairs in Labour politics. But it was enough to persuade many of the members of the local party to stay away from the selection process at the end of 2003. What happened there made matters worse. The success-ful candidate was Maggie Jones who now found herself suspected for practically every attribute that in other circumstances might have counted in her favour. Welsh-born, yes, but Cardiff? Father a miner at Oakdale? Fair enough, but for how long? Trade union official? OK, but which union? And the gravest of her crimes, it appeared, were her membership of the Labour Party's National Executive Committee and her personal friendship with Tony and

Cherie Blair. If you lived in Blaenau Gwent, it was felt, you didn't have to be Hercule Poirot to work out that she was a New Labour crony, parachuted into the district to make it safe for the right wing. In this way it was possible to shift the argument from the delicate matter of all-women shortlists to the manner in which authority had been ripped from the hands of the local party to serve the interests of some remote metropolitan caucus. Now they could say that the problem wasn't that the new candidate was a woman, but that she was this specific woman.

The key figure who brooded over this issue for a long time was Peter Law, the Assembly Member for the constituency, someone who had held elected office for Labour for more than 30 years. He might well have been a candidate himself but, under the imposed restrictions, he could not even be considered. His carefully-phrased argument was, naturally, that while everyone wanted to see more women MPs the people of Blaenau Gwent should have the freedom to pick on merit anyone they wanted to be their representative. No one should be imposed upon them. This wasn't a matter of gender but of democracy.

The big problem for the Labour Party centrally was that Peter Law was a dangerous character. He was a man with a grievance. When the assembly had begun its life in 1999 he was an leading figure, a member of the original Cabinet. The following year, though, he was one of those pushed out to make way for a Liberal Democrat as the First Minister, Rhodri Morgan, gave up his efforts to continue minority government and formed a coalition. Law, always an opponent of proportional representation, was outraged. In conversation he made no attempt to disguise his hostility to Rhodri whose Cabinet he believed to contain a number of inadequates who owed their positions solely to their loyalty to the First Minister. Nor was he an admirer of Rhodri's own administrative skills.

Another rebuff made matters worse. For the 2003 election the assembly's Deputy Presiding Officer, John Marek, was deselected by his local constituency Labour party in Wrexham but nevertheless won when he stood as an independent. Law stood for the job of Deputy Presiding Officer but lost when some Labour members supported Marek instead, an expedient move to help with the delicate party balance in the assembly. What price loyalty now Law might well have asked.

As time passed it became increasingly likely that Law would

stand, but as an experienced politician he was careful not to confirm the speculation. The Labour Party began to get worried. Would he like to be Deputy Presiding Officer after all? Or perhaps Presiding Officer, it was tentatively suggested? Perhaps such things could be arranged. Law himself, it was believed, thought that something further up the scale should be considered. A return to the Cabinet, perhaps, and a promise that he could stay there. Whatever the details of the discussions no deal could be done. Politicians and analysts began to make calculations. It seemed pretty certain that if there were to be a by-election he'd win the seat. But at a general election it would surely be more difficult. And there was also the emotional question of breaking with a party he had served for so long. In a conversation we had at the end of 2004 I suggested to him that if he won he'd be in for a difficult life; he'd be very lonely at Westminster. "I'm used to that in Cardiff," he said.

In Ebbw Vale on Monday, April 4, 2005, he called a press conference at which he had intended to announce that he would be standing as an independent at the general election, to be held on May 5. Instead he told the reporters and cameras something entirely different. The previous morning he had collapsed at home. In the afternoon a brain tumour had been diagnosed. Later that day he'd be going to the University Hospital of Wales in Cardiff for further investigations. In the circumstances...

Down at Transport House in Cardiff, Labour officials went round being sympathetic. Get well soon, Peter, they said, and we'll put this little difficulty behind us. Since the crime of opposing the party remained uncommitted, no problem would arise – 'the door is open' – he could remain in the party if he chose.

Which he didn't. Less than a fortnight after a six-hour brain operation he was telling the *Western Mail* that he was now making a very good recovery. He'd been 'overwhelmed' by messages urging him to fight the seat. "I am giving very serious consideration to the idea of standing," he said. Oh, and by the way, he'd resigned from the Labour Party.

When he did decide to stand, Labour did what parties often do when in a panic: the wrong thing. In a series of responses that made it clear they thought Law would win, Blaenau Gwent was faced with the orchestrated arrival of senior politicians sent out to defend a vast Labour majority in a place where, four years before, they'd won 72 per cent of the vote. David Blunkett appealed to

him to "do the big thing and stand aside". Gordon Brown wrote a
letter to every household saying it would be difficult for Peter Law
to represent the constituency effectively at both Westminster and
Cardiff Bay. He passed over the fact that, among others, both Alun
Michael and Rhodri Morgan, the two first First Ministers had
done exactly that between 1999 and 2001.

And in case it wasn't absolutely certain that the seat would be
lost, the Deputy Prime Minister, John Prescott, added his weight
to the impending disaster when he visited another part of the
county. What did he think of Peter Law's decision? he was asked
by Mark Choueke, a reporter from the *South Wales Argus*.

"It didn't even register with us," Prescott replied. "It's unfor-
tunate that some of our decisions upset some people."

The reporter persisted. Prescott told him: "Why are you
asking me about this? I don't care. It's a Welsh situation. I'm a
national politician."

In the best foot-in-door traditions of his trade, Mark Choueke, as
the *Argus* reported, was undeterred. Did the Deputy Prime Minister
think he was too big to care about the voters of Blaenau Gwent?

"Where do they get these amateurs from? You're an amateur,
mate. Go get on your bus, go home."

Was Mr Prescott too big for the regional press, then?

"Bugger off. Get on your bus, you amateur."

Incidents of this kind may give us a glimpse of the reason why
Mr Prescott's attempts to bring devolution to other parts of the
United Kingdom have met with an unsympathetic response from
the voters. But in the case of Blaenau Gwent it's unlikely that
anything he could have said, even if he'd been overwhelmed by a
rare conciliatory moment, would have influenced the final result.
On May 5, 2005, what had been a Labour majority of more than
19,000 in a place that had been at the very core of the party's solidarity for a century, became overnight a majority of more than
9,000 for an independent candidate.

As his supporters cheered, fifty-seven-year-old Peter Law
stood on the platform at the Ebbw Vale leisure centre, his head
partly shaved, revealing the scars of his recent operation. He told
the crowd: "The people rose up because their integrity was being
compromised by New Labour. It became a crusade and people
wanted their dignity and self-respect to be recognised."

Was that what the vote really meant? Up to a point, obviously, that was the case. But people who like politics for their own sake appreciate results of this kind because they defy the momentum of the system. It's impossible not to enjoy the grinding noise the party machine makes when someone decides to throw his spanner into it. Who can fail to take pleasure when an individual triumphs over the organisation? What independent spirit could fail to laugh some months later when Peter Law won an award as Welsh politician of the year and Labour members present at the televised ceremony suddenly became seized with the urgent need to read copies of a political directory rather than applaud him? Later, some of them preferred to make jokes about his illness, which clearly still affected him. But then, at the same ceremony another politician, to show his disapproval of her views on Iraq, ostentatiously refused to applaud Ann Clwyd. Politicians often say they admire independence of spirit but what they like above all other things is people who agree with them.

Behind all this, though, the question remained of whether the arresting political outcome of Peter Law's intervention had a wider significance. Well, it was certainly one of those rare examples of voters deciding they weren't going to be taken for granted, that there was a limit to the extent to which they were prepared to be messed about in the name of party loyalty. And it had happened before, not very far away.

In Merthyr Tydfil in the nineteen-sixties Labour decided that it was time for their MP, S.O. Davies, to stand down. After all, they argued with some justice, he was already eighty years old when he won it in 1966 and he had been the member since 1934. Surely it was now time for a dignified retirement? S.O. (he was always known by his initials and, indeed, always referred to himself by them, in the third person) disagreed. The party deselected him and put in his place Tal Lloyd, a well-known and very able official of the engineering workers union. As it happened at that time there was some disaffection with the AEU because of its handling of a major dispute at the Hoover factory, one of the most important local employers. This might well have influenced the outcome. Four years earlier S.O. had won the seat for Labour with a majority of more than 17,000. Now he retained it as an independent with a majority of more than 7,000.

This result was clearly comparable to what happened in Blaenau Gwent thirty-five years later and for a while it seemed it

might have significantly disturbed the political ecology of industrial South Wales, When S.O. died two years after his last election,
at the age of eighty-six, the Labour candidate at the by-election,
Ted Rowlands, fought it as if it were a marginal. It was a sensible
precaution. Plaid Cymru, in that period getting some spectacular
results in the valleys, came within fewer than 4,000 votes of
winning. Two years after that, though, Rowlands had a majority of
more than 13,000 and from then on it was as if nothing had ever
unbalanced the political equilibrium of the district.

Perhaps Blaenau Gwent will eventually reach very much the
same position, although Labour's decision to expel twenty
members for their parts in the Peter Law affair (in some cases very
minor parts indeed) will probably make the healing process more
protracted that it would otherwise have been. But the truth is that,
once again, it was chance rather than any tide of history that had
the main influence in this compelling episode. It seems certain that
only Peter Law could have brought about this result. If he hadn't
been sacked from the Cabinet to make way for a Liberal
Democrat; if his own party had supported him for the job of
Deputy Presiding Officer; if it hadn't been possible to portray
Maggie Jones as descending on Blaenau Gwent by parachute; If
there hadn't been the awkward fact that all-women shortlists
hadn't been imposed in Scotland; if the Labour Party organisation
had been generally a bit more alert and diplomatic the election of
2005 might have taken a very different course. But that is how it
works. At a time when large areas of political life are characterised
by bloodless consensus, the fact that the unpredictable can still
spring out from the shadows is a cause for celebration.

The celebrations didn't last long. Chance, fate, whatever you like
to call the forces that reveal how little control individuals have over
their own destinies, hadn't quite finished their intervention in this
remarkable story. Peter Law's brain tumour hadn't been cured. In the
early months of 2006 even the fierce, single-minded passion that had
given his personal political cause so much vigour could no longer
compete with his declining health. On April 25, almost exactly a year
after he'd left a hospital bed to administer a peremptory lesson to his
old party, he died at home at the age of 58. The precise nature and
extent of the lesson he delivered was at that moment unclear, except
for one thing: that sometimes, even in modern, manufactured politics, the individual can still make a difference.

One last question remains. Was this affair really about the right of people to make their own decisions, in Peter Law's words, because they wanted their dignity and self-respect to be recognised? Or was it because they simply didn't want a woman MP, imposed or otherwise? Both, is almost certainly the answer. And in this, as we know, the Labour voters of Blaenau Gwent are no more reactionary than those Tory selection committees in the Home Counties. In the end, though, this isn't an argument about gender but about lives turned upside down. Occasionally people, in furious frustration, seize an opportunity to push some intolerably offensive manifestation of the modern world down the hill, like a boulder. In Blaenau Gwent in 2005 it was a declaration of independence as deeply informed by the people's historic hostility to the imperatives of outsiders – owners, nationalised corporations, the Labour Party's National Executive – as was Arthur Scargill's doomed attempt to lead the miners to revolutionary triumph.

Conservatives like history too. After all, that's been one of the main attributes that has defined the party. So the extraordinary phenomenon that was Margaret Thatcher takes her place as a useful aberration, an abrasive and unexpected interlude in a long narrative of emollient self-interest. We're not really like that you know, they suggest as they ditch their madcap flirtation with egalitarianism. Those provincial grammar school people, Heath, Thatcher, Hague and Howard, were a long experiment that didn't work out. More than forty years after Sir Alec Douglas-Home had twenty-one public schoolboys, including eleven Old Etonians, in his Cabinet, party members recognised that it was time to turn once more to class, even if class is no longer quite what it was. Give us another Old Etonian, David Cameron, and the voters will soon be seduced before his effortless superiority. That was the old-fashioned message. The Tory rank and file had never had a proper vote before and when they got one they turned their backs on the glitter of novelty. And who can blame them? After all, Labour has enjoyed its two greatest periods of success – 1945-1951 and from 1997 onwards – under two public schoolboys, Clement Attlee and Tony Blair.

The long dominance of Blair and the unexpected arrival of Cameron are two things no one would have predicted in the middle of the nineteen-eighties when, between them, Arthur and Maggie seemed to have established the future course of British political life for a generation. Accidents, misjudgements, misunderstandings and flaws of character were among the many things that led to that final struggle. We couldn't say then that the tide of history was so inexorable that it would inevitably have swept away the stones and swamped the rocks that stood in its way. Nor can we say it now. 'What if?' applies as much to the future as it does to the past.

BIBLIOGRAPHY

Abse, Leo: *Private Member* (Macdonald, 1975)

Adonis, Andrew & Thomas, Keith (eds): *Roy Jenkins, A Retrospective* (Oxford, 2004)

Page Arnot, R: *The Miners: Years of Struggle* (George Allen & Unwin, 1953)

Page Arnot, R: *The South Wales Miners 1914-1926* (Cymric Federation Press, 1975)

Beddoe, Deirdre: *Out of the Shadows, A History of Women in Twentieth Century Wales* (University of Wales Press, 2000)

Campbell, John: *Nye Bevan and the Mirage of British Socialism* (Weidenfeld & Nicolson, 1987)

Castle, Barbara: *The Castle Diaries 1964-1976* (Papermac, 1990)

Cosgrave, Patrick: *Margaret Thatcher, a Tory and her Party* (Hutchinson, 1978)

Crossman, Richard: *Diaries of a Cabinet Minister, Vol. 3 Secretary of State for Social Services 1968-70* (Hamish Hamilton & Jonathan Cape, 1977)

Eyre, Richard: *National Service: Diary of a Decade at the National Theatre* (Bloomsbury, 2004)

Foot, Michael: *Aneurin Bevan Volume 1: 1897-1945* (Macgibbon & Kee, 1962)

Foot, Michael: *Aneurin Bevan Volume 2 1945-1960* (Davies-Poynter, 1973)

Francis, Hywel & Smith, Dai: *The Fed, A History of the South Wales Miners in the Twentieth Century* (new edition, University of Wales Press, 1998)

Gormley, Joe: *Battered Cherub* (Hamish Hamilton, 1982)

Hattersley, Roy: *Who Goes Home?* (Little, Brown, 1995)

Healey, Denis: *The Time of My Life* (Michael Joseph, 1989)

Jenkins, Roy: *A Life at the Centre* (Macmillan, 1991)

Lee, Jennie: *My Life With Nye* (Jonathan Cape, 1980)

Llewellyn, Richard: *How Green Was My Valley* (Penguin Classics, 2001)

McAllister, Laura: *Plaid Cymru The Emergence of a Political Party* (Seren, 2001)

MacGregor, Ian (with Rodney Tyler): *The Enemies Within* (Collins, 1986)

Massingberd, Hugh (ed): *The Daily Telegraph Book of Obituaries, A Celebration of Eccentric Lives* (Macmillan, 1995)

Massingberd, Hugh (ed): *The Daily Telegraph Fifth Book of Obituaries, 20th Century Lives* (Pan, 1999)

Masson, Ursula: *Florence Rose Davies (1882-1958) Independent Labour Party Activist, Labour Alderman* in Keith Gildart, David Howell and Neville Kirk (eds): *Dictionary of Labour Biography, Vol. XI* (Palgrave Macmillan, 2003)

Morgan, Kenneth O: *Callaghan: A Life* (Oxford University Press, 1997)

Mortimer, John: *In Character* (Penguin, 1984)

Neil, Andrew: *Full Disclosure* (Pan, 1997)

Price, Lance: *A Spin Doctor's Diary: Inside Number 10 With New Labour* (Hodder and Stoughton, 2005)

Seldon, Anthony: *Blair* (The Free Press, 2005)

Thatcher, Margaret: *The Downing Street Years* (Harper Collins, 1993)

Walker, Peter: *Staying Power* (Bloomsbury, 1991)

Westlake, Martin & St. John, Ian: *Kinnock* (Little, Brown, 2001)

Whitehead, Philip: *The Writing on the Wall, Britain in the Seventies* (Michael Joseph, 1985)

Wilson, Harold: *Final Term, The Labour Government of 1974-76* (Weidenfeld & Nicolson and Michael Joseph, 1979)

Young, Hugo: *One of Us*, Final Edition (Macmillan, 1991)

INDEX

ABOUT THE AUTHOR

Patrick Hannan's career as a writer, journalist and broadcaster includes periods as a newspaper reporter, an industrial correspondent, thirteen years as the BBC's Welsh political correspondent, a television producer and a radio presenter. He has been a regular contributor to Radio 4 for well over twenty years and since 1998 has been half the Welsh team on *Round Britain Quiz*. He currently presents two regular series on Radio Wales. He has also been a newspaper columnist and has contributed to a wide variety of UK newspapers and magazines.

His other books published by Seren are *The Welsh Illusion, Wales Off Message* and *2001 A Year In Wales*.

PATRICK HANNAN

THE WELSH ILLUSION

Wales has changed almost beyond recognition in the last twenty years, yet many still cling to the romantic image of what it once was rather than cope with the reality of what it has become. The persistence of myth in the face of incontrovertible evidence is one of the Welsh illusions addressed in this book. Another is the conjuring trick through which a new Wales has been discovered, and sometimes created, by politicians, broadcasters, journalists and historians. Patrick Hannan explores these changes and their origins, and describes how in the process so many people have been abruptly separated from their past. He does so in part through the stories of individuals, famous and unknown. How Sir Anthony Hopkins' grim schooldays prepared him for his most celebrated role; the belated arrival of the twentieth century in Aberystywth; Chuck Berry and the death of deference; the rampant tribalism of the South Wales Valleys; Sir Winston Churchill's part in inventing Welsh politics; the venom that lay behind Viscount Tonypandy's apparently boundless Christian goodwill: these are some of the leads followed up by Hannan in search of his country.

The Welsh Illusion is a provocative and entertaining contribution to the understanding of how Wales reached its present condition and where, under its new and evolving system of government, it may be going.

ISBN 1-85411-368-2   £8.95

PATRICK HANNAN

WALES OFF MESSAGE

"On October 27, 1998, Ron Davies became the first Cabinet Minister ever to resign for not doing anything wrong."

"Under the plumed Cavalier's hat of Rhodri Morgan's verbal dazzle he wears the iron helmet of a member of Cromwell's New Model Army."

"Rod Richards is a man who can denounce ten things before breakfast and then eat three Shredded Wheat."

"If they had given out medals for the 1979 devolution campaign, Alun Michael would have clanked round in his all day, like Corporal Jones in Dad's Army."

From Ron Davies's "moment of madness" to a Lib-Lab pact the new Welsh assembly had fraught beginnings. Patrick Hannan scrutinises the sagas of Ron and Alun and Rhodri and Rod, placing them in the complicated context of the organisations and people who set the agenda of public life in Wales. The humiliating failure of Labour's attempts to control Wales from London; Plaid Cymru's anti-independence stance; inter-party manoeuvring in the Assembly; trouble for the Welsh establishment at its club; increasing difficulties for the monarchy; these are the strands which make the state of Wales. This is a compelling story about both Wales and Britain, and one which, as Hannan discovers, is also richly comic.

ISBN 1-85411-293-7   £8.95

www.seren-books.com

Patrick Hannan
2001: A Year in Wales

As Patrick Hannan watches the events of 2001 unfold and describes them in this chronicle of a year in Wales the sound of laughter is rarely far away, despite the seriousness of events. The result is a revealing picture of the kind of country Wales now is, its obsessions, its ambitions, its divisions, and the nature of the people who run it or want to run it. The fury over English views of the Welsh and Welsh views of the English; the huge gap between aspiration and achievement when it comes to erecting buildings or playing rugby; political jealousies and the private agenda behind public events are among the ways in which the nature of modern Wales is explored.

ISBN 1-85411-314-3 £8.95

www.seren-books.com